P9-DME-785

Rennay Craats

WEIGL PUBLISHERS INC.

Published by Weigl Publishers Inc.
123 South Broad Street, Box 227
Mankato, MN, USA 56002
Web site: http://www.weigl.com

Library of Congress Cataloging-in-Publication Data available upon request from the publisher. Fax (507) 388-2746 for the attention of the Publishing Records Department.

ISBN 1-930954-29-8

Printed and bound in the United States of America
1 2 3 4 5 6 7 8 9 0 05 04 03 02 01

ıenior Editor
ared Keen

Series Editor
Carlotta Lemieux

Copy Editor
Heather Kissock

Layout and Design
Warren Clark
Carla Pelkey

Photo Research
Joe Nelson

Photograph Credits

Archive Photos: pages 3B, 7BL, 7BR, 8, 15, 17T, 18, 22, 23, 24, 25, 28, 29, 30, 31T, 31B, 41, 42, 43; Bettmann/CORBIS: pages 14B, 19T, 39T; Tim Boxer/Archive Photos: page 14T; CF Peters Corporation: page 27; Deutsche Presse Agentur/Archive Photos: pages 6BL, 16; Frank Driggs/Archive Photos: page 40; Hemera Studio: page 34; Shel Hershorn, UT Auston/Archive Photos: pages 3MR, 38; Hulton-Deutsch Collection/CORBIS: page 17B; Hulton Getty/Archive Photos: pages 20BR, 21; NASA: pages 6BR, 9, 26; National Archives of Canada: page 36BR; Popperfoto/Archive Photos: page 37; Roz Payne/Archive Photos: page 32; Photofest: pages 3TL, 10, 11, 12, 13; United States National Archives and Records Administration: pages 20TL, 35; Weight Watchers International: page 33.

Contents

USA 1960s Introduction

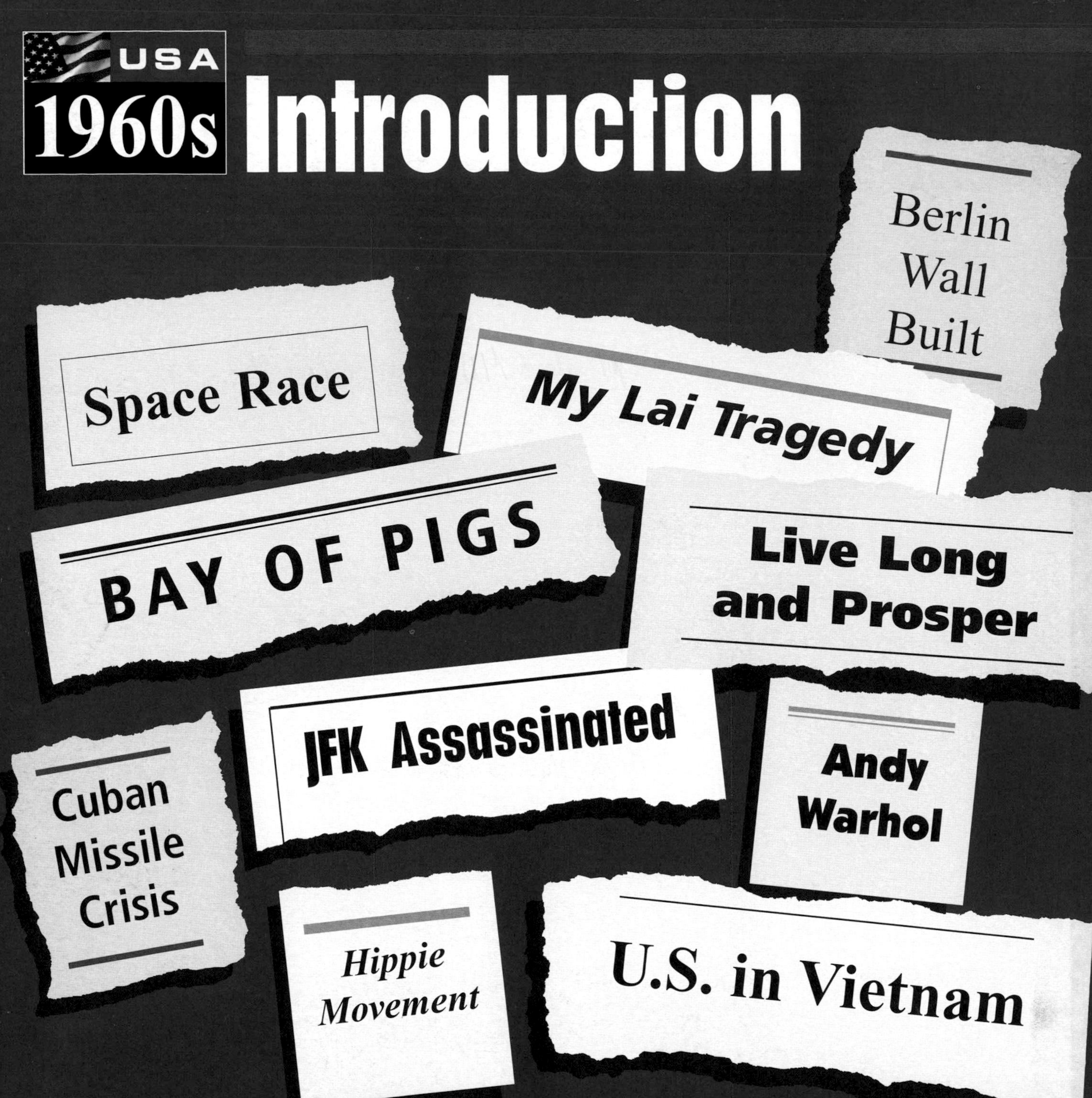

The sixties were a time of change and protest. Across the country, people demonstrated for the end of war and racial discrimination. These gatherings were not always peaceful.

Television became an important way in which to learn about events. In 1960, millions of Americans watched presidential candidates square off in televised debates. John F. Kennedy won the debates and the election, becoming a very popular president. His assassination devastated the country. Many Americans can remember where they were when they heard the news of Kennedy's death. It was the end of an era.

During the 1960s, many colonies in Africa became independent countries. In 1961, the Soviet Union sent a man into space. Sometimes television brought its audience amazing images. In 1969, about 600,000 million people watched Neil Armstrong become the first person to step on the moon.

Breakfast at Tiffany's

Eichmann Captured

Six-Day War

Beatles Invade

Gulf of Tonkin

To Kill a Mockingbird

Thalidomide Pulled

DR. KING SHOT

Beach Boys

Americans also watched the Boston Celtics win eight straight National Basketball Association championships. They cheered as the Chicago Blackhawks claimed the Stanley Cup, and they gaped at the footage of half-a-million young people who had gathered for three days of peace, love, and music at Woodstock. Each of these events have become cornerstones of history.

Not every story could be covered in *20th Century USA: History of the 1960s*. Some stories were chosen because they played an important role in shaping history. Others appear because they represent the people and experiences of the time.

Your local library has old newspapers and magazines filled with stories from the sixties. CD-ROMs and the Internet are great places to learn more about this decade. For now, sit back, turn the page, and experience the "groovy" history of the sixties.

USA 1960s Time Line

1960

Hollywood goes psycho for horror movies. Anthony Perkins and Janet Leigh terrify Americans with an Alfred Hitchcock twist. Page 10 has the scoop on this controversial hit.

1960

The Congo celebrates independence in 1960. But the road is a bumpy one. Flip to page 18 to learn more about Belgium's withdrawal and the fight for control of the area.

1960

A plane crash in the Soviet Union causes serious strife. Americans watch as a spy drama unfolds. Find out what happened on page 42.

1961

Freedom Riders take to the streets to test a Supreme Court ruling. They find that the ruling really does not change the racial climate in the country. Find out why on page 33.

1961

Roger Maris swings his way into baseball history. His home-run record remains unbroken for thirty-seven years. To read more about this incredible athlete, turn to page 28.

1961

East Germany is fenced in, due to the Berlin Wall. Miles of concrete separate the East from the West. To learn more about this legendary wall, turn to page 16.

1961

"Hail to the Chief" never sounded better than it did to John F. Kennedy that November. He took his place in the White House to the excitement of millions across the country. Find out why he stirred up so much fervor on page 20.

The Berlin Wall

1962

Her movies, style, and whispery voice made her a legend, and now the most beautiful woman in Hollywood is dead. The country is stunned by the blonde bombshell's passing. To find out more about Marilyn Monroe, turn to page 10.

1962

A dispute over nuclear weapons brought the world to the brink of war. The **Cold War** got colder in October as the Soviet Union and the U.S. faced off over nuclear missiles in Cuba. Turn to page 21 to find out how the tensions were resolved.

1962

Americans tune in via satellite as AT&T launches Telstar. Page 26 has more on this scientific marvel.

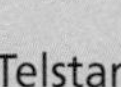

Telstar

1963

An American hero is gunned down during a parade in Dallas. President John F. Kennedy's death devastates the country and leaves questions unanswered. Read more on page 21.

1963

Life is wild for Maurice Sendak. His children's books thrill readers and impress critics. Find out about his exciting literature on page 24.

1963

Elizabeth Taylor is crowned Queen of the Nile. Page 12 has more about Cleopatra, Taylor, and Richard Burton.

1964

The civil rights movement gets a boost when the Civil Rights Act is passed. While it is a step in the right direction, it is not enough to calm the tensions and violence in the country. Turn to page 22 to find out why.

1965

U.S. military personnel switch from being advisors to active participants in the Vietnam War. Read about America's involvement in a costly and controversial war on page 23.

1965

Raised hemlines raise eyebrows as the miniskirt hits the fashion scene. Page 37 has more about this revolutionary design and the country's reaction to it.

1965

Immigration receives an overhaul as the Immigration Act is introduced. Find out how policies change on page 39.

1965

All eyes are on Broadway Joe. He passes up the National Football League to join the American Football League. Learn the outcome of his decision on page 29.

1966

After an appeal, Americans were given the right to remain silent. Arrested suspects are now protected by the Miranda ruling. Find out who Miranda was and what the courts decided on page 22.

1966

Sci-fi lovers are told to live long and prosper every week through television. Read about the amazing series that captivated the world on page 12.

1966

The University of Austin campus is held hostage. Sixteen die and thirty-one are wounded at the end of the nightmare. Turn to page 8 to read more about the sniper in the tower.

1967

Six days of war sweep the Middle East in the summer of 1967. Find out what caused the conflict and how it ended on page 19.

1968

The whole world watches the Democratic Party's national convention in Chicago. The city erupts as demonstrations turn violent. Read more on page 8.

1968

The man who advocated peace is gunned down in Memphis. The death of Martin Luther King, Jr., leaves a void in many Americans' hearts and in the civil rights movement. Page 33 has more about this extraordinary man.

1969

Neil Armstrong is out of this world—literally. He touches down on the moon on July 21 to the amazement of millions of people. Turn to page 27 to find out more about his historic journey into space.

1969

Three days of peace, love, and music turn into the most famous concert in history. Find out how half-a-million young people make do on a New York farm on page 41.

The Vietnam War

Star Trek

Many people were outraged at the actions of the police during the Democratic Convention.

Demonstration Disaster

The 1960s were filled with huge protests and demonstrations. Sometimes these gatherings turned violent. On August 23, 1968, 10,000 people met at the Democratic Party's national convention in Chicago. They gathered to protest racism, the war in Vietnam, and the government that allowed these things to happen. They demanded peace. About 20,000 police officers and soldiers were called in to keep order. They brought out batons to fight the rock-throwing protesters. They also attacked some journalists and passersby. As police clubbed the protesters with batons, other demonstrators chanted, "The whole world's watching." Television cameras captured the scene for the six o'clock news broadcasts. The cost of the clash was high—about 700 protesters and eighty police officers were injured, and 650 demonstrators were arrested.

Six days later, demonstrators marched to the convention amphitheater to be heard. Security officers were nervous and quick to attack. As well as hitting protesters, they scuffled with delegates and newspeople. Walter Cronkite, a popular news anchor who openly opposed U.S. involvement in Vietnam, called the officers "thugs." The violence surrounding the Democratic convention threw the party into turmoil and further divided the country.

Tower Sniper

Twenty-five-year-old Charles Whitman's life unraveled on July 31, 1966, when the ex-Marine killed his mother and his pregnant wife. The next day, he headed to the University of Austin campus armed with a bag full of sandwiches, a radio, seven guns, and hundreds of rounds of ammunition. There, Whitman climbed to the observatory tower, killing three people on the way. From the top of the tower, he began to fire on the students below.

Every available police officer rushed to the campus. They were virtually helpless—Whitman shot anyone who tried to help the injured and anyone who came out in the open. His military training ensured that he was an accurate shot. His bullets were not just aimed at the campus. A man a few hundred yards away at a newsstand was gunned down as well. Whitman shot in all directions, leading police to think there were several gunmen in the tower. After about an hour-and-a-half, police stormed the tower. Two police officers and a former air force officer made it into the building. They reached the top of the tower and shot Whitman. When the massacre was over, sixteen people lay dead and thirty-one were wounded. The sniper's action devastated Texas and the rest of the country. The tower has been closed, reopened, and closed again over the years.

My Lai Tragedy

On March 16, 1968, three platoons of the 11th Brigade, American Division, moved through a South Vietnamese village called My Lai. They had been sent on a search-and-destroy mission as part of the Vietnam War—they were to look for enemy soldiers and kill them. The troops did not find **Vietcong** soldiers. Instead, hundreds of unarmed Vietnamese citizens, including elderly men, women, and children, were killed. Estimates of the number of dead ranged from 109 to 567 people. There was only one American casualty at the end of the assault. A U.S. soldier had shot himself in the foot so he would not have to take part in the massacre. An army helicopter pilot later reported the large number of dead civilians below, but division investigators ruled that nothing unusual had occurred at My Lai.

In April 1969, Ronald Ridenhour, a member of one of the platoons, claimed that war crimes had been committed that day. The U.S. Army began another investigation, and the truth about the massacre became known. Platoon Lieutenant William Calley was charged with 102 counts of murder. He was convicted and sentenced to life in jail. His sentence was soon reduced to twenty years and then again to ten years. The actions of U.S. soldiers in My Lai created more negative public opinion about the Vietnam War in the U.S.

Apollo Nightmare

On January 27, 1967, three astronauts arrived at Cape Canaveral, Florida, for a routine training exercise. Virgil Grissom, Edward White, and Roger B. Chaffee were rehearsing for the first *Apollo* flight when tragedy struck. During a practice countdown, a flash fire swept through their spacecraft. The fire spread quickly because the craft was filled with pure oxygen. All three astronauts burned to death. The launching crew was watching the exercise on television monitors. They saw a flash of light and then a great deal of smoke. The fire was so hot, rescue workers could not get close enough to the craft to extinguish the flames. These three men were the first astronauts to die. The cause of the fire was unknown, and it put in question President Kennedy's promise of reaching the moon in this decade.

The world mourned the loss of the three astronauts that were to make the first trip to the moon—Virgil Grissom, Edward White, and Roger Chaffee.

Entertainment

Loss of a Legend

On August 5, 1962, Americans mourned the loss of the most idolized screen legend in history. Marilyn Monroe was found dead at the age of thirty-six. She had captivated magazine and movie audiences with her beauty since the 1940s. Monroe became a superstar in the 1950s when she starred in such movies as *There's No Business Like Show Business* (1954), *The Seven-Year Itch* (1955), and *Some Like it Hot* (1959). She married baseball hero Joe DiMaggio in 1954 and divorced him the following year. A year later, Munroe married playwright Arthur Miller and acted in his films, including her last movie in 1961, *The Misfits*. She divorced Miller shortly after the film was released. While the nation was taken by Marilyn Monroe's appearance, she focused on her own imperfections. She craved security but could not find it. In 1962, Monroe's involvement with drugs and alcohol, along with deep depression, led to her being fired from the set of a movie. Only a month later, she was found dead in her home from an overdose. Books, movies, and collections of photographs continue to be produced about the life of Marilyn Monroe decades after her death.

Marilyn Monroe will be remembered forever in the hearts of Americans.

The Girl in the Rubber Mask

Carol Burnett got her break as a regular on the *Garry Moore Show* in the 1950s. Burnett won Americans' hearts by making them laugh out loud at her klutzy manner and crazy facial expressions—*TV Guide* called her "the girl in the rubber mask." After leaving the show, Burnett toured and hosted specials. She won an Emmy Award for a special with Julie Andrews. Then, in 1967, she was given her own show. Over its eleven-year run, *The Carol Burnett Show* featured comedians Harvey Korman, Tim Conway, Vicki Lawrence, and Lyle Waggoner. The combination of hilarious skits and a live audience sometimes spelled trouble for the actors. At times, they struggled to keep a straight face and continue with the program. This made audiences love the show even more. In 1978, Burnett decided to end the series. *The Carol Burnett Show* remains one of the most successful variety shows ever produced.

PSYCHO

The 1960 thriller *Psycho* terrified theater audiences, but many critics were not impressed. They felt that director Alfred Hitchcock had gone too far. The film was about Norman Bates, played by Anthony Perkins, who seemed like a quiet motel keeper. In reality, he dressed in his dead mother's clothing and killed unlucky visitors staying at the inn. Bates murdered a young woman, played by Janet Leigh, as she took a shower. His stabbing of her stands as one of the most frightening scenes in movie history. Despite critics' claims that the movie was sadistic, *Psycho* was a box office smash, winning Janet Leigh a Golden Globe award for her performance. Today, the movie is praised for its sophistication, complexity, and scariness.

Trailblazers

When Sidney Poitier came to New York, he was laughed out of an audition, but he was not discouraged. He returned six months later and landed a role with the American Negro Theater. He starred in his first movie, *No Way Out*, in 1950. *The Defiant Ones* (1958) brought him his first Academy Award nomination. Then, in 1963, Poitier became the first African American to win a Best Actor Oscar, in *Lilies of the Field*. Poitier starred in more than forty films throughout his career,

including *Guess Who's Coming to Dinner*, *To Sir With Love*, and *In the Heat of the Night*. Poitier's success laid the groundwork for other African-American actors in the film industry.

Bill Cosby was another trailblazing African American. In 1965, he became the first to star

Sidney Poitier was an active civil rights supporter. His controversial movies promoted equal rights for everyone.

in a weekly television show. *I Spy* broke television's racial barrier, featuring all actors as equals. Cosby won Best Actor Emmy Awards for his performances in 1966, 1967, and 1968. He went on to host his own comedy-variety show called *Cos*. He also starred in several television series including *The Cosby Mysteries* and *The Cosby Show*, and he created the award-winning cartoon series *Fat Albert and the Cosby Kids*.

Breakfast with Audrey Hepburn

Audrey Hepburn left Europe for Hollywood to become an actor. She was immediately welcomed as a star after her performance in *Roman Holiday* (1953). The movie was a hit, and she won an Academy Award. Hepburn found success with several other movies in the fifties, but in 1961 she became a legend when she played Holly Golightly, a symbol of beauty and femininity, in *Breakfast at Tiffany's*. Her character was the queen of small talk at cocktail parties and was a walking contradiction. Golightly was an independent woman, but she relied on others and wanted to be cared for at the same time. She lived the big-city life but was a small-town girl at heart. Her appeal on the screen meant a smash at the box office and another Best Actress Academy Award nomination.

Three years later, Hepburn starred in *My Fair Lady* with Rex Harrison. Professor Henry Higgins, played by Harrison, makes a bet that he can transform street vendor Eliza Doolittle, played by Hepburn, into an upper-class lady by teaching her to change the way she talked and behaved. In the process, the professor and his student fall in love. The movie was another hit, and it won eight Academy Awards. In 1967, Hepburn was again nominated for an Academy Award for her performance in *Wait Until Dark*. After retiring at the end of the sixties, the Hollywood idol became a goodwill ambassador for the United Nations International Children's Emergency Fund (UNICEF).

DICK VAN DYKE SHOW

While the show took a while to catch on, it became a television classic. *The Dick Van Dyke Show* claimed a spot on television's top ten and stayed there for nearly its entire five-year run. The show followed the lives of comedy writer Rob Petrie, played by Dick Van Dyke, his wife Laura, played by Mary Tyler Moore, and their friends. The episodes recapped the couple's courtship, the problems encountered when trying to write funny material for a variety show, and the wacky home lives of the Petries. Americans loved the show, and they hated to say goodbye to it, but the cast wanted to explore other opportunities. In its last season in 1966, Dick Van Dyke, Mary Tyler Moore, the show's writers, and the show itself won Emmys.

Sci-Fi Show Lives Long and Prospers

"Our mission: to boldly go where [no one] has gone before."
Star Trek theme

In 1966, U.S. television audiences were introduced to a science-fiction series, but low ratings suggested that most viewers did not really notice. *Star Trek* was a show about the crew aboard the starship *Enterprise* in the 23rd century. Unlike many shows of the time, *Star Trek* was ethnically representative of society—the show starred an African American, an Asian, and a Scot. The series boasted the first interracial (and interspecies) kiss on television. In the three years that *Star Trek* appeared on network television, it never rated higher than number fifty. Worldwide ratings, however, were a very different matter. The show found an enthusiastic following outside of the U.S. The seventy-nine original episodes gave rise to several films, more than a hundred novels, a cartoon series, and later spin-off series, including *The Next Generation*, *Voyager*, and *Deep Space Nine*.

The fanatic followers of the series, called Trekkies or Trekkers, created an entire subculture around the series. They published newsletters, learned the alien languages created on the show, and attended *Star Trek* conventions dressed as characters from the show. Many people were drawn to *Star Trek* by the mind-boggling technology of the future, including transporters that "beamed" people to other locations.

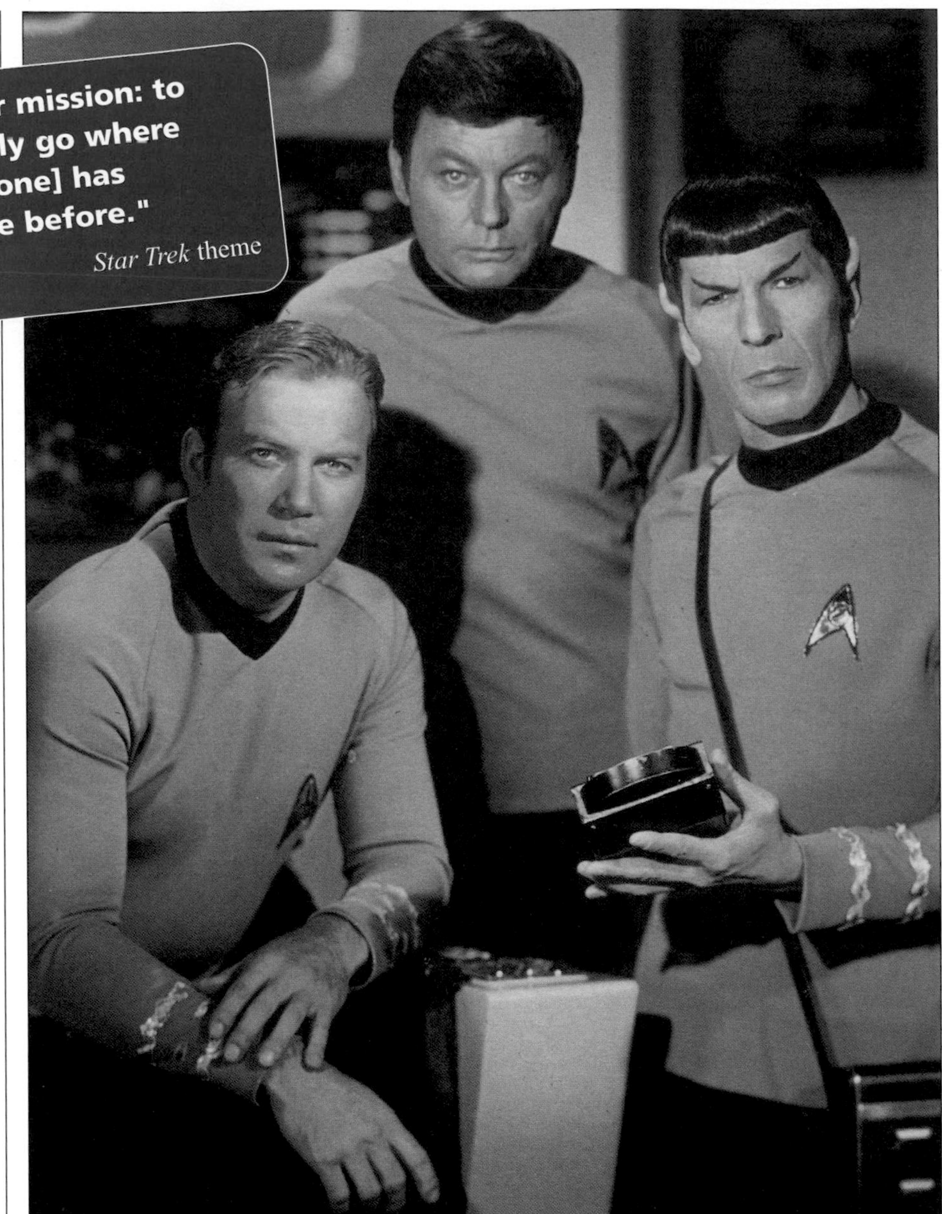

The hi-tech world of *Star Trek* has drawn millions of viewers since its creation in 1966.

ELIZABETH TAYLOR THE QUEEN

In 1963, Elizabeth Taylor became royalty. She starred as the Queen of the Nile in *Cleopatra*. For this role, she was paid the unheard-of salary of $1 million. No other star had been paid that much to act in a movie before. *Cleopatra* was the most expensive movie ever made up to that time. Despite the money put into it, the movie flopped at the box office. This failure did not take the spotlight off Taylor, though. The on-set attraction between her and co-star Richard Burton had Americans' undivided attention. The two married in 1964, becoming Hollywood's favorite couple. But the fairytale did not last long. They divorced a few years later, remarried, and then divorced again. This was only one of Taylor's many highly public marriages and divorces over the next several decades.

Funny Girl

At 21 years old, Barbra Streisand seemed like a veteran on Broadway, even though she had starred in only one production before *Funny Girl*. On March 23, 1964, she brought the role of Fanny Brice, a comic diva, to life. Streisand had much in common with her character—they were both Jewish girls from New York, they both admitted to having an odd sense of humor, and they both possessed enchanting looks. Most of all, both stars had an unbelievable **rapport** with the audience. Streisand took twenty-three curtain calls after debuting in the part. She played the role again in 1968 on the big screen and was just as successful. She won an Academy Award for her performance. Despite her success, Streisand could not overcome her stage fright. Even after she conquered acting, singing, directing, and composing, her fear of performing in public stayed with her. She avoided live concerts as much as she could until 1994, when she began to appear in public more often.

Laugh-In

The comedy team of Dick Martin and Dan Rowan introduced the U.S. to *Rowan & Martin's Laugh-In* in January 1968. It was a variety show with a twist—it featured skits, sight gags, crazy songs, and the invitation to "Sock it to me." Every week, the cast stuck their heads out of doors and windows on the Joke Wall to deliver funny lines. There was a weekly party scene, and everyone would freeze while someone delivered a joke, and would then resume dancing once the punchline was delivered. The show made fun of politics and social issues, which was uncommon in sixties television. It also featured surprise guests, including politicians and celebrities. *Laugh-In* was the number one show for its first two seasons, and it gave stars such as Goldie Hawn and Lily Tomlin their start. Some of the phrases used on the show became part of Americans' everyday language in the sixties.

***The Sound of Music* was based on the true story of the von Trapp family.**

Sound of Success

The recipe for success in the 1960s included an Austrian family that sang a lot, a nanny, and a country at war. *The Sound of Music* told the story of a family of nine in Austria who make a daring escape from Nazi territory to the safety of Switzerland. The movie, which starred Christopher Plummer as a wealthy captain and Julie Andrews as the nanny with whom he falls in love, is one of the most-watched movies ever produced. But this was not immediately the case. The movie opened to mixed reviews in 1965. Then the public showed its support by rushing to theaters in droves to watch the film. It set a new box-office record, beating out the previous record holder, *Gone with the Wind. The Sound of Music* also cleaned up at the Academy Awards, winning for Best Picture, Best Director, Best Film Editing, Best Sound, and Best Musical Score.

Pop Art

Popular art, or pop art, began in response to abstract art in the 1940s and 1950s. Pop artists thought art should be drawn from real life. Their works were inspired by popular culture. While this style had existed in the fifties, it developed quickly in the sixties. One American artist built funny representations of fast food. Another reconstructed comic book frames using oils. Then Andy Warhol, who became a leading artist in the popular art revolution, took the genre a step further. He produced hundreds of works using silk-screening. His pictures of such everyday items as Campbell's Soup cans, Coca-Cola bottles, and Brillo Soap Pad boxes delighted Americans. Warhol also mass-produced silk-screens of celebrities, including Marilyn Monroe, in many different colors. His exhibitions were instant sensations across the country. Warhol's experiences as a commercial illustrator opened the door for him to explore this unique form of art. Pop art not only had an impact on the art community, it also had an effect on commercial, graphic, and fashion design in the 1960s.

Andy Warhol's vision continues to influence modern art.

Twisting

In the 1960s, all a dancer needed was music. Partners were optional. A dance called the twist had been popular in the African-American community, but it took Chubby Checker to bring it to the rest of the country. This 20-year-old singer recorded "The Twist" and performed it on the television show *American Bandstand*. Then Americans from all areas of the country took up twisting. It became a number-one hit with both teenagers and adults. Soon, spin-off songs and dances popped up, including the peppermint twist, the mashed potato, and the frug. Other popular dances were the hitchhiker, the monkey, and the jerk. All of these dances brought light-hearted fun and enthusiastic dancers to dance floors across the country.

New styles of dancing appeared throughout the decade.

Hippie Movement

The hippie movement became strong in many parts of the U.S., especially in the Haight-Ashbury district of San Francisco. Hippies saw themselves as separated from their parents' generation and did all they could to show it. They were not concerned with material goods and often shopped at second-hand stores or army surplus stores. To them, clothing was a necessity, not a sign of wealth. To further escape from and put down Western **capitalism**, they wore ethnic clothing. Many wore tribal patterns and styles borrowed from Eastern countries. Hippies followed Eastern philosophies and religions, some of which involved meditating. They made love beads and other ethnic jewelry popular. Through their actions, hippies tried to encourage peace and love, and they fought for social issues, including civil rights and the withdrawal of troops from Vietnam. Although the hippie movement represented only a small percentage of the U.S. population, its ideals and styles filtered into mainstream society.

Hippies rebelled against the mainstream through their clothes, hair, and beliefs.

Slang

freak out react strongly to something

fuzz the police

groovy great

man name for everyone, male or female

psychedelic vivid or bold, involving the abstract

rip-off unfair deal or circumstances

Hats Off to Hair

Big really was beautiful in the 1960s, at least where hair was concerned. Women spent hours in front of their mirrors, with curlers, combs, and hair lacquer close at hand, trying to achieve the right height. First, they teased their hair with combs to give it the desired volume and sprayed it heavily to hold its shape. Then they lifted the top layer of hair over the teased hair and sprayed it in place. This gave the hairstyle its height and hive shape. Many women washed their hair only once a week. They kept the style in place by wearing carefully placed curlers at night and reteasing and spraying in the morning. The beehive style, which was a carry-over from the fifties, remained popular until the mid-sixties.

Women who could not or did not want to wear a beehive often went for the bouffant look. Their hair was still full, but it was not pulled back into the final beehive shape. Women with this hairstyle still teased and sprayed to achieve the perfect look. First Lady Jacqueline Kennedy wore a toned-down bouffant hairdo and made this style a fashion must. With such large and elaborate hairstyles, most women left their hats at home. Those who wore hats chose ones that were big enough to fit over their huge hairdos, or they chose tiny pillbox hats that sat on top of the head.

WAR CRIMINAL CAPTURED

A long search finally came to an end on May 11, 1960. Israeli secret agents arrested a man in Buenos Aires who later identified himself in court as Adolf Eichmann. Eichmann had been the chief of the **Gestapo's** Office of Jewish Affairs during World War II. He had helped organize the **Holocaust**, right down to choosing the poison the Nazi's used in the gas chambers. Since 1945, Eichmann had lived under false names in countries that had been sympathetic to the Nazi cause.

War crimes investigators found Eichmann and brought him to justice. During the four-month trial in Jerusalem, survivors of the Holocaust and witnesses to Eichmann's part in it testified how he had planned the murder of millions of people. In his own defense, Eichmann said he was only following orders. His argument did not help him avoid a guilty verdict. He was hanged for his crimes on May 31, 1962.

Other Side of the Wall

On August 13, 1961, East German troops started to put up a fence of barbed wire between East and West Germany. The wire was soon replaced by concrete walls and electric fences aimed at keeping East Germans in. What became known as the Berlin Wall was guarded by minefields, dogs, and soldiers.

Between 1949 and 1961, more than 2.5 million East Germans had escaped from the hard times of their **communist** country, mostly through West Germany. Early in 1961, the Soviets suggested that Allied troops withdraw from Berlin. The West refused, because it wanted to prevent the communists from taking over. Soviet leader Nikita Khrushchev threatened to use nuclear weapons to enforce his demands. Fearing serious problems, 30,000 East Germans defected in July. To prevent any more from leaving, the communists built the Berlin Wall. Travel into East Germany was monitored, and travel from East to West Germany was out of the question. The Wall stayed intact for nearly thirty years. About eighty people died trying to cross over to West Germany.

The 26-mile-long Berlin Wall stretched through the city, separating families.

Prague Spring

The communist government in Czechoslovakia hired several intellectuals to come up with a way to improve the country's economy. The intellectuals came to realize that if economic reforms were to work, there had to be political reforms, too. In January 1968, a pro-reform member of the Communist Party became the country's new premier. Alexander Dubcek introduced dramatic reforms, which included the ability to form opposition parties in government, as well as the freedom of the press. Such liberties had been restricted ever since the Soviet Union took control of the country after World War II. But this freedom did not last. On August 20, Soviet troops arrived. Residents put up a nonviolent resistance, including switching street signs to confuse the soldiers. Dubcek was removed from power, and Soviet troops regained control over the area. Over the next several years, Czechoslovakian leaders would not discuss reform because they feared a repeat of the Prague Spring.

Tanks roll through the streets of Prague, bringing with them a return to hard-line communism.

Space Race

In the 1960s, the Soviet Union came out ahead of the U.S. in the space race. On April 12, 1961, **cosmonaut** Yuri Gagarin became the first man in space. He had been a military fighter pilot so was no stranger to demanding, challenging missions. He broke the ties of gravity and became the first to fly in space. He spent 108 minutes orbiting Earth in the spaceship *Vostok*. Gagarin returned a hero. People in the Soviet Union were stunned when they heard of his death in 1968. He had crashed while test-piloting a MIG-15 fighter plane.

"I want to dedicate this first cosmic flight to the people of Communism—the society which the Soviet people are now already entering upon."

Yuri Gagarin, before his historic flight

The Soviet Union had two more firsts in the sixties. The *Vostok 6* took the first woman, Valentina Tereshkova, into space two years after Gagarin paved the way. She made forty-eight revolutions around Earth in just under seventy-one hours in June 1963. Tereshkova had volunteered for space-flight training school and was trained as an airplane pilot there. Then, on April 15, 1965, Alexei Leonov became the first person to walk in space. He left the spacecraft for ten minutes, floating alongside it. This Soviet success in space only spurred the Americans on. Four years later, an American would walk on the moon.

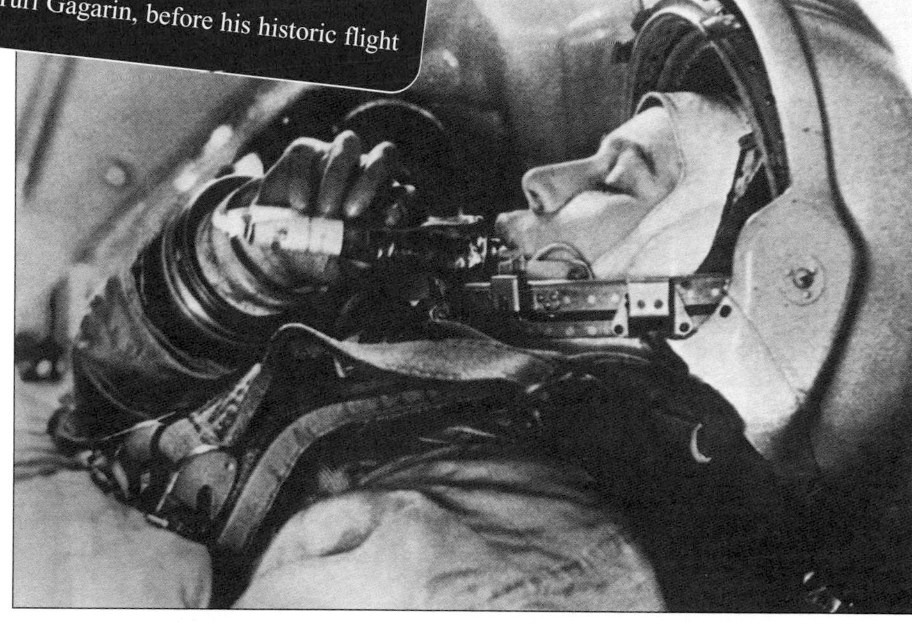

Valentina Tereshkova prepares for her three-day voyage into space.

Algerian War

Independence did not come easily for Algerians. It took eight years of intense fighting with France before Algeria became an independent nation. The battle started in 1954, with attacks and counterattacks that killed thousands. By the time of the 1962 truce, 17,000 French troops had died, and up to a million Algerians had been killed. French President Charles de Gaulle tried to negotiate peace, but he failed. His proposed reforms were not accepted by the colonists and were considered insufficient by Algerians. A referendum showed that voters approved the peace treaty of 1961, but some colonists rebelled. De Gaulle fought against these rebels and arrested the leaders. In 1962, peace talks took place as bombs continued to explode in both Algeria and France. On July 5, 1962, Algeria's independence was official. A brief civil war and new elections placed a neutral **socialist** government in power. As French settlers left the area, some destroyed hospitals, libraries, and factories. The Algerian war was one of the longest and most violent independence struggles ever fought between a European power and a colony.

Algerian women protest the persecution of their families at the hands of the French army. Most Algerians were opposed to French rule.

Conflict in the Congo

The Belgian Congo was an unstable place, and Belgian officials knew it. Native Africans had been given no control or participation in government. In June 1960, Belgium held elections and, fearing rebellion from nationalists, quickly granted the country independence. The Belgian Congo became the Republic of the Congo. Almost immediately, dozens of different ethnic groups in the country began fighting for control, and the army **mutinied** against its Belgian officers.

Belgium backed the mineral-rich province of Katanga's bid to become the next government. The United Nations stepped in, sending about 20,000 mostly African soldiers to help the government establish order. Within three months, the situation had stabilized, but the government had splintered. President Joseph Kasavubu and Premier Patrice Lumumba wanted to take the government in different directions and disagreed on how to run the country. In September, a Kasavubu supporter named Colonel Joseph Mobutu took over control of the Congo. He worked on fighting Katangan efforts to gain control of the government. In November 1965, Mobutu led another **coup** and claimed leadership for himself. This brought about a new era of fighting in the Congo.

Rhodesia Splits

Members of the Zimbabwe African National Union gather to protest British support of the white minority government in Rhodesia.

Northern Rhodesia gained independence from Britain in 1964. Southern Rhodesia gained independence in 1965. The two countries had radically different plans for the future. Northern Rhodesia was granted independence as the Republic of Zambia. It had a population of more than 3.6 million and was led by Kenneth Kaunda. Kaunda tried to soothe resentment toward non-African citizens, who numbered about 75,000. He also tried to ease minorities' fears of a black government. The developments in Rhodesia and South Africa made Kaunda nervous. The hostility and domestic unrest due to poverty prompted him to bring about a one-party state in 1972. After nearly twenty years, he legalized opposition and retired in 1991.

Southern Rhodesia, led by Ian Smith, became the nation of Rhodesia. Smith refused to allow African ministers in his government or to extend rights to African citizens. Smith's government brought international sanctions and civil war to the area. In 1978, after years of war, Smith agreed to appoint African ministers and give blacks the right to vote. He stepped down as prime minister in 1979, and Rhodesia became the independent, majority-rules country of Zimbabwe the following year. Smith kept his seat in Parliament until 1987.

Six-Day War

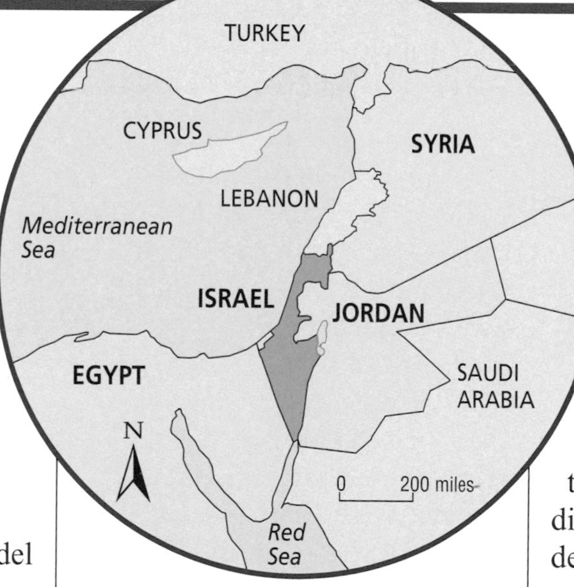

The Middle East is a politically charged area. Conflicts have been erupting there for centuries.

Israel and its neighbors—Jordan, Syria, and Egypt—had clashed since the 1940s, when Israel became a nation. Its neighbors had refused to recognize Israel and had attacked the new country, but Israel drove them back. In 1956, Israel attacked Egypt in the Suez-Sinai War, and the Egyptian president, Gamal Abdel Nasser, promised revenge. In April 1967, Syria attacked Israeli villages, so Israeli forces shot down six of Syria's Soviet-made fighter planes. When Egypt then joined forces with Syria, war seemed unavoidable.

On June 5, 1967, Israel decided to launch a surprise attack. Its planes destroyed 309 of 340 Egyptian aircraft, and its ground troops then drove Egyptian forces from the Sinai Peninsula and Gaza Strip. Meanwhile, Jordanian troops attacked Israel from the east. Israeli planes hit back and largely destroyed Jordan's fighter planes. Its ground troops attacked Jordan's troops in Jerusalem, and the Israelis claimed the whole city.

Israeli planes continued to attack Arab air bases, disabling most of its enemies' air defenses. Ground battles in Sinai and the West Bank pushed Arab forces out and Israelis in. Israeli forces also pushed Arabs out of the Golan Heights. By June 10, Israel and Syria had agreed on a cease-fire. While in theory the war was over, fighting between the countries continued for many years.

President John F. Kennedy delivers his victory speech after the 1960 election.

BAY OF PIGS

In 1960, the Central Intelligence Agency (CIA) began training a secret force of Cuban **exiles**. The plan was to have the 1,500-member force invade Cuba at the Bay of Pigs. The exiles were to gain Cuban support and overthrow the Communist government of Premier Fidel Castro. It was to appear as a Cuban coup, not an American invasion. On April 17, 1961, the soldiers set sail for Cuba. Within three days of attacking, more than 100 of them were dead, and the rest were taken prisoner. The CIA had thought the attack would cause an uprising in the country, but that did not happen. Most Cubans supported Castro and his government, so they did not help the exiles. In the end, the U.S. paid a $53 million ransom in food and medicine for the men's release. The failed invasion embarrassed the Kennedy government and the CIA.

Kennedy Control

In the 1960 election, presidential debates were held on television for the first time. Millions of Americans watched candidates John F. Kennedy and Richard Nixon debate the issues. Kennedy won the debates and the election. At 43 years old, Kennedy was the youngest person to become president of the U.S. and the first Catholic to hold the post. When he took office in 1961, he set out to strengthen the economy and moved toward **desegregating** the nation. During his time as president, Kennedy fought communism and promoted American growth.

His achievements in the White House were only a part of why the country loved him. Kennedy's two young children added a family feel to the presidency. Caroline and John, Jr. were the youngest children to live in the White House in more than sixty years. The nation also adored Kennedy's wife, Jacqueline, and people across the nation copied her style. The Kennedy family was admired both for its charm and its devotion to the U.S.

Cuban Missile Crisis

The U.S. and the Soviet Union had never had direct, armed conflict during their power struggle. In the 1960s, a hostile relationship between the countries' leaders had the world bracing for nuclear war. In 1961, the Soviet Union based missiles in Cuba within easy firing distance of the U.S. This was the first time they had set up nuclear weapons in the Western Hemisphere. President Kennedy ordered a blockade of Cuba on October 22, 1962, and he announced to Americans that his forces were ready for anything. While the Soviet government did not challenge the blockade, it refused to remove weapons already in Cuba. Kennedy sent 200,000 U.S. soldiers to Florida, ready for war. A U.S. pilot flying **reconnaissance** over Cuba was shot down—but he was the only casualty of the crisis. On October 28, Nikita Khrushchev agreed to remove Soviet missiles from Cuba, and the U.S. agreed to remove its missiles from Turkey. The world breathed a sigh of relief as the anticipated World War III was averted.

A U.S. patrol plane keeps watch over a Soviet freighter during the Cuban Missile Crisis.

PEACE CORPS ESTABLISHED

President Kennedy was dedicated to battling issues facing developing countries. Even before he became president, he had thought up a plan for a volunteer organization that would send people overseas to help those in need. They would work as teachers, agricultural specialists, doctors, and nurses in poor countries. On November 2, 1960, less than a week before the presidential election, Kennedy proposed the creation of a Peace Corps. By autumn 1961, the first volunteers were in the field. By the 1990s, the Peace Corps was working in over 100 countries in Africa, Latin America, Asia, Eastern and Central Europe, the Pacific, and the Mediterranean.

JFK Assassinated

A single shot silenced the nation during a parade on November 22, 1963. President Kennedy, his wife, and Texas Governor John Connally and his wife were driving down a Dallas street in a convertible. Admirers gathered to get a glimpse of the president and first lady. As the car neared the Texas School Book Depository, the sound of gunfire rang out. President Kennedy slumped in his seat—he had been fatally shot. Disbelief and panic swept the scene as the convertible raced off toward the hospital. A citizen filming a home video had the only recording of the assassination. It was analyzed and reanalyzed so that investigators could piece together the tragedy.

Twenty-four-year-old Lee Harvey Oswald was arrested for the deed. Police said he had shot the president from the sixth floor of the depository. Many people were not convinced that Oswald had carried out the assassination on his own, but investigators did not have much time to talk to him. Two days later, as he was being moved from a city jail to a county one, Jack Ruby shot and killed Oswald at close range.

Many people insisted there was a conspiracy—some said Cuban leader Fidel Castro had arranged the assassination, others blamed the CIA, the KGB, or the Mafia. The official, although controversial, finding was that Oswald had acted alone. Regardless of who planned it, Kennedy was dead. The country mourned the loss of its leader and what could have been. Lyndon B. Johnson was sworn in three hours later and took over as president.

Miranda Warning Becomes Law

In 1963, Ernesto Miranda was arrested, and after two hours of police questioning, he confessed to kidnapping and rape. He was later convicted. His lawyer **appealed**, saying that Miranda had confessed because he was frightened by police. Therefore, his statement should not have been allowed at trial. The Supreme Court overturned Miranda's conviction in 1966.

The judges ruled that police officers had to tell suspects about certain rights before they were arrested and questioned. If officers did not, the prosecution could not use anything at the trial that had been said during the investigation. Any additional evidence that police found because of the statements was also disallowed. The Miranda ruling said that suspects must be informed of the right to have a lawyer and the right not to say anything **incriminating**, and they must be told that anything they said could be used by prosecutors to convict them. Police departments across the country have followed the ruling ever since. Miranda was retried and was convicted without using his confession.

"You have the right to remain silent. Anything you say may be used against you in a court of law."

Part of the Miranda warning

Gulf of Tonkin Resolution

In 1964, U.S. forces returned fire after two **allegedly** unprovoked North Vietnamese attacks were launched against U.S. army destroyers. As a result, Congress authorized President Johnson's request for emergency powers with the Gulf of Tonkin Resolution. This resolution allowed him to become involved in Vietnam and stop the spread of communism. He could take any measures to defend Americans. The law also meant that U.S. forces could elevate the fighting without officially declaring war. Not all senators supported the law. They felt it gave the president too much power and too much room to expand that power.

Despite some opposition, Johnson moved into Vietnam. He assumed that North Vietnamese forces would fall to even a minimal American attack. What he did not consider was the troops' determination. U.S. troops became players in what would be a long and costly battle. In 1971, a leaked report called the Pentagon Papers suggested that the Americans attacked the North Vietnamese to draw their fire. By reporting that the Vietnamese had fired first, the report suggested, Johnson was able to gather support for his military actions.

Civil Rights Act Passed

The civil rights movement swept the nation in the sixties. Tensions were high and conflicts often turned violent as the country's 22 million African Americans demanded equal rights. After the death of three civil rights workers in Mississippi, public outrage gave Johnson the support he needed to pass the 1964 Civil Rights Act, which had first been proposed by Kennedy. This made it against the law to refuse people accommodation because of their race, or to ban them from voting lists, employment, unions, and federally funded programs. Southern senators fought against the law, but they could not stop it from passing. It was the most extensive civil rights bill in U.S. history. Still, conflict and violence continued across the country, and African Americans struggled to make the spirit of the Act a reality in practice.

Thousands gather in front of the Washington Monument during the Freedom March for civil rights.

The first U.S. soldiers to arrive in Vietnam march along a beach near the U.S. Army base in Danang.

Taking Aim in Vietnam

In 1965, U.S. military bases were attacked in Vietnam. The U.S. military went from advising South Vietnam to actively fighting in the war. The number of U.S. troops in the area reached 154,000. U.S. and South Vietnamese troops went on search-and-destroy missions of Vietcong. But military success destroyed villages and often caught civilians in the crossfire. As the year wore on, B-52 bombers, carrying 58,000 pounds of bombs, blasted the important North Vietnamese strongholds of Hanoi and Haiphong. Before this, Americans had not targeted these areas because they did not want to draw the Soviet Union and China into the conflict. There did not seem an end in sight for the Vietnam War. By 1967, there were 525,000 U.S. troops in Vietnam.

ANOTHER LOST HERO

In 1968, the Kennedys mourned the loss of another family member. John F. Kennedy's brother Robert had been shot in a hotel after delivering a speech. Senator Robert Kennedy was against the Vietnam War, so he decided the best way to stop it was by trying to get the Democratic Party nomination. He began down the campaign trail that he hoped would end at the White House. Kennedy gained strong support during his campaign. On June 5, Kennedy was leaving a victory celebration in Los Angeles when Palestinian American Sirhan B. Sirhan shot him. The assassin was protesting the U.S. alliance with Palestine's enemy, Israel. Kennedy died from his wounds the next day. He was buried near his brother John in Arlington National Cemetery.

LBJ All the Way

In 1964, Lyndon B. Johnson was elected to a full term as president. His victory was the largest popular majority in modern American history. He aimed at creating a "Great Society," which would help the economically and politically poor. Johnson pushed for **urban renewal**, health care, and education for all Americans. He was also a dedicated patriot and vowed to maintain American commitments around the world. This included Vietnam. His policies in Vietnam were controversial, and his efforts to end the war failed. In 1968, his announcement to step down as president shocked the country. The U.S. was divided by the Vietnam War, and Johnson said that he did not want the presidency to become involved in this division. Richard Nixon won the election to become the thirty-seventh president of the U.S.

"Aggression unchallenged is aggression unleashed."

President Johnson

Literature

In Cold Blood

Truman Capote's nonfiction novel was an instant hit and created a new kind of writing called literary journalism, or creative nonfiction. The first 100,000 copies of *In Cold Blood* (1966) sold out almost immediately. Americans wanted to get their hands on the gritty, reconstructed account of the murder of the wealthy Clutter family from Kansas. Capote dug into the lives of the Clutters, allowing readers to get to know them before they were murdered on November 14, 1959. With the help of his childhood friend Harper Lee, he interviewed people in the community, the Clutters' friends, and—most importantly—the killers themselves, to put together the puzzle of how and why the murders took place. Capote spent six years gathering information, conducting interviews, and writing *In Cold Blood*. He also became involved in the lives of the killers, Perry Smith and Dick Hickock. He followed their sentence all the way to the electric chair.

Truman Capote was a well-known writer and socialite.

ROLLING STONE

In 1967, Jann Wenner borrowed $7,500 from his uncle and started a magazine with 52-year-old columnist Ralph Gleason. The magazine was aimed to appeal to the rock-and-roll youth culture, which was growing strong in the U.S. On November 9, Wenner's magazine, *Rolling Stone*, debuted on newsstands. John Lennon appeared on the first cover wearing a World War II British army helmet. Within the first two years, *Rolling Stone* reached a circulation of 64,000 subscribers. It featured regular articles by such sixties idols as writer Hunter S. Thompson. By 1987, *Rolling Stone*'s circulation hit more than 1 million, and it remained a popular publication into the 21st century.

Wild About Maurice

Maurice Sendak knew what children were afraid of—he had once been a kid himself. He wrote and illustrated books that explored what children feared and fantasized about—getting lost, being bullied, and being in charge. Sendak was an illustrator first, adding pictures to such books as *The Wonderful Farm* (1951) and *A Hole Is to Dig* (1952). Then, in 1956, he wrote and illustrated *Kenny's Window*. He had become known in children's literature, but in 1963, he became famous with the classic *Where the Wild Things Are*. He won the Caldecott Medal the following year for the bestseller. It was one of three books in a series. The others, *In the Night Kitchen* (1970) and *Outside Over There* (1981), were also successful. Sendak won the Hans Christian Andersen International Medal in 1970 and the Laura Ingalls Wilder Award in 1983. Later, he designed the sets and costumes for an opera based on his stories.

American Takes Nobel Prize

Many of John Steinbeck's novels were set around his home state of California. He understood the life that fruit pickers lived because he had been one as a young man. Several of his works, including *Pastures of Heaven* (1932) and *In Dubious Battle* (1936), focused on just such a farming community. *Tortilla Flat* (1935) was the first Steinbeck novel to be praised by critics and the public alike. One of his best known novels was *The Grapes of Wrath* (1939). It followed the lives of the Joad family during the Great Depression. In 1961, Steinbeck published *The Winter of Our Discontent*, and the next year he was honored with the Nobel Prize for Literature. His impressive list of novels dating back to the 1920s earned him success and recognition on an international level. His concern for people spurred him to become a war correspondent during the Vietnam War in 1966 and 1967, much as he had during World War II. Several of Steinbeck's novels were made into movies, and his works have become required reading in many high school and university literature classes.

John Steinbeck was a humanitarian and a celebrated literary master.

To Kill a Mockingbird

Harper Lee's experience in law school shone through in her 1960 novel *To Kill a Mockingbird*, but her novel was more than a courtroom drama. It was the story of a small-town, Caucasian lawyer and his efforts to make sure an African-American man wrongly accused of rape received a fair trial. It was told from the point of view of a six-year-old girl named Scout as she watched her father, lawyer Atticus Finch, fight for justice. In the novel, racial tensions explode in the Alabama town before and during the trial. The novel reflected U.S. life and quickly became a bestseller. Lee won the Pulitzer Prize for Fiction in 1961, and her words were brought to life on the big screen in 1962. The film version, starring Gregory Peck, won Academy Awards for Best Writing, Best Actor, and Best Art Direction. The film and the novel have become American classics.

WORLD FOCUS

DAHL DAZZLES READERS

Children around the world welcomed more Roald Dahl books in the 1960s. The British writer had found success with novels, short stories, and scripts, but he was best known for his children's books. He joined the Royal Air Force and fought in World War II. While fighting in the war, Dahl wrote his first children's book, **The Gremlins** ***(1943). First Lady Eleanor Roosevelt loved the story and read it to her grandchildren. She invited Dahl to the White House, and the Roosevelts and Dahl became friends. The book became a popular movie in 1984. One of Dahl's most famous stories is*** **James and the Giant Peach** ***(1961). His focus on children's literature came from having children himself. He figured that if he had not had children, he would never have thought of writing the wonderful stories he produced. He continued thrilling young readers with such books as*** **Charlie and the Chocolate Factory** ***in 1964. Dahl's talent in entertaining was rewarded with many prizes, including the Federation of Children's Book Groups Award, the World Fantasy Convention Award, and the Edgar Allan Poe Award from the Mystery Writers of America.***

Science & Technology

Television in Space

In 1962, AT&T sent the first communications satellite into orbit. *Telstar* floated 500 to 3,500 miles above Earth. It received faint television signals, magnified them 10 billion times, and then sent them back to Earth. This allowed television audiences in the U.S. to receive programs from Europe, and Europeans to receive U.S. programming. The implications of what *Telstar* could do caused great debate over future satellites and ground stations—would the government develop high-orbit satellites and own the skies, or would AT&T be allowed to continue with its low-orbit satellites? To come out ahead of the Soviets in telecommunications, President Kennedy decided to back AT&T, making the company more successful than ever before.

Satellites changed the art of communication technology.

SPACE HEROES

On February 20, 1962, an American entered space aboard the spacecraft *Friendship*—John Glenn was the first American to circle the Earth. He orbited three times in less than five hours as Americans sat glued to their television sets watching him, but it was far from a perfect mission. Instead of firing small jets to keep the spacecraft in position, *Friendship* was firing large jets—and using up fuel that was needed to get home. Then ground station readings suggested that the craft's heat shield had been detached. This meant that *Friendship* and Glenn would burn up upon re-entering Earth's atmosphere. To overcome these problems, Glenn switched to manual-control systems to stop the big jets from firing. The worries about the heat shield proved false, and he landed safely in the Atlantic Ocean.

In June 1965, astronaut Edward White became the first American to walk in space. For twenty-two minutes, White floated in space attached by a cord to the *Gemini 4* capsule. He used a gun that fired bursts of compressed oxygen to propel himself in the weightlessness of space. The flight commander, James McDivitt, took pictures of the historic moment. The astronauts returned to Earth as heroes.

WORLD FOCUS

THALIDOMIDE PULLED FROM MARKET

Around the world, thalidomide was called "the sleeping pill of the century." What people did not know was how dangerous it was to unborn children. Pregnant women who took the drug put their unborn children at risk. Thalidomide caused up to 12,000 babies to be born disabled throughout the world. Many of these children died soon after birth. Other babies were born with flipper-like limbs instead of arms and legs. Often, their ears, eyes, and internal organs were also damaged. The drug was pulled from the market in 1962, but the harm had been done.

In the U.S., only about a dozen children were affected, thanks to Frances Oldham Kelsey, an FDA investigator. She turned down the drug after reading that it caused nerve ***inflammation*** *and did not always aid in sleeping. She faced pressure to accept the drug for more than a year, but she refused. Even though the drug was not approved, some U.S. doctors got free samples from the makers. About 20,000 female patients in the U.S. used the drug. Once the world realized the disastrous effects of the drug, Kelsey was awarded a medal by President Kennedy.*

Keyboard Music

Milton Babbitt was a mathematician who turned his knowledge of numbers and formulas to music. He was one of the first people to use computer technology to study the structure of music. In 1959, Babbitt helped establish the Columbia-Princeton Electronic Music Center. His "Composition for Synthesizer" (1961) was one of the first pieces of electronic music. Other works include "Philomel" (1964) for soprano and magnetic tape, and "Concerti for Violin, Small Orchestra, and Synthesized Tape" (1976). Babbitt decided to use certain pitches, harmonies, and rhythms beforehand, and created what he called "total serialization" in his music. He was honored with a Pulitzer Special Citation for his work in 1982.

Milton Babbitt is a highly honored composer.

The Eagle Has Landed

> **"That's one small step for man, one giant leap for mankind."**
> Neil Armstrong, from the moon

About 600 million people watched on television as astronauts broadcast their transmissions from the moon. As John Kennedy had promised, Americans visited the moon before the end of the decade. On July 16, 1969, Michael Collins, Neil Armstrong, and Edwin "Buzz" Aldrin, Jr., boarded the *Apollo 11* and headed for the moon. Four days later, Aldrin and Armstrong climbed into the landing craft called the *Eagle* to complete their trip to the moon. The astronauts were surprised by the huge boulders on the moon's surface but successfully touched down. Armstrong stepped out first onto the powdery surface of the moon, kangaroo-hopping around in the low-gravity atmosphere. Aldrin joined him nineteen minutes later. For more than two hours, they collected samples, set up instruments that would monitor the atmosphere, and planted a U.S. flag to show they were the first to explore the moon. Armstrong and Aldrin reluctantly returned to their spacecraft and headed back to Earth. They safely splashed into the Pacific Ocean off the coast of Hawaii on July 24 and took their place in the history books.

Scoring Machine

Wilt Chamberlain is thought to be one of the greatest basketball players in the history of the National Basketball Association (NBA).

Throughout his 14-year professional career, Chamberlain claimed 23,924 rebounds and scored 31,419 points. The only player to score more was Los Angeles Lakers center Kareem Abdul-Jabbar.

In 1959, the 7-foot-1-inch-tall Chamberlain was the star of the University of Kansas basketball team. He graduated and moved directly onto the squad of the NBA's Philadelphia Warriors. For his first seven seasons, he led the league in scoring. On average, he scored fifty points a game. On March 2, 1962, Chamberlain set an incredible record. He scored 100 points in a game against the New York Knicks.

The superstar was traded to the Philadelphia 76ers in 1965 and to the Los Angeles Lakers in 1968. He continued to lead his team and the league. With Chamberlain at the helm, the Lakers won the 1972 NBA title. Chamberlain was added to the Basketball Hall of Fame in 1978.

Wilt Chamberlain set many records throughout his career. He was the only NBA player to score 4,000 points in a season.

HEAVY HITTING

New York Yankee Roger Maris was no stranger to home plate. His team came to expect their outfielder to hit home run after home run. In 1961, Maris hit his sixty-first home run in the last game of the season. Nobody had ever hit that many home runs in a single season. To go along with this impressive record, Maris was named the American League's Most Valuable Player in 1960 and 1961. In 1966, the left-handed slugger was traded to the St. Louis Cardinals, and he retired from the game in 1968. His record remained unbroken for thirty-seven years. In 1998, the St. Louis Cardinals' first baseman Mark McGwire blasted seventy home runs during the regular season.

Broadway Joe

In 1965, the University of Alabama's star quarterback Joe Namath shocked the country. He snubbed the National Football League to join the New York Jets of the new American Football League. To show how happy they were about his decision, the Jets gave their starter a contract worth $400,000. It was the highest-paying professional sports contract ever at the time. Namath proved that he was worth every penny. He promised fans that he would lead his team to the 1969 Super Bowl, and he did. He was named the Most Valuable Player and won the S. Rae Hickok award as the athlete of the year. In the off-season, Namath launched his acting career. He appeared in several films and television programs throughout his athletic career. This interest earned him his nickname, Broadway Joe.

Namath retired from football in 1978, but he stayed involved in the sport through television broadcasting. His knowledge and strong personality made him a star. Namath was inducted into the Pro Football Hall of Fame in 1985.

Olympic Statement

The racial tensions in the U.S. carried over into the 1968 Olympic Games in Mexico City. Two African-American athletes, Tommy Smith and John Carlos, competed in track and field.

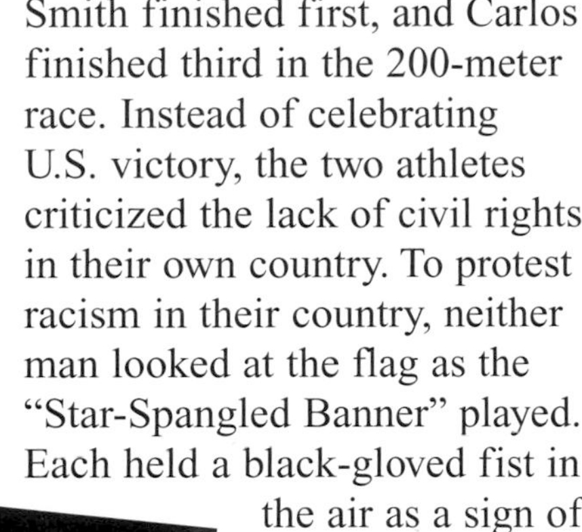

Smith finished first, and Carlos finished third in the 200-meter race. Instead of celebrating U.S. victory, the two athletes criticized the lack of civil rights in their own country. To protest racism in their country, neither man looked at the flag as the "Star-Spangled Banner" played. Each held a black-gloved fist in the air as a sign of Black Power. Their statement did not impress the U.S. Olympic committee. The men were suspended from the Games and were ordered to leave Olympic village immediately. The image of the defiant men on the podium became a symbol of racial discontent in the sixties.

Tommy Smith and John Carlos raise a fist to express feelings about race relations in the U.S.

BLACKHAWKS WIN THE CUP

The Montreal Canadiens had won five Stanley Cup hockey championships in a row from 1956 to 1960. It seemed as though they were unstoppable. Unstoppable, that is, until Bobby Hull and the Chicago Blackhawks came along. The team had not won a championship title since 1938, and they were due for a big victory. That victory came in 1961, when Hull's blazing speed and incredible slap shot proved too much for the Canadiens. The Blackhawks managed to do what no other U.S. hockey team could do in the 1960s—they won the Stanley Cup. They have not won a championship since, but many of the team's players have set impressive league records. In 1960 and 1962, Bobby Hull was the top scorer in the league. From 1964 to 1968, a Blackhawk held the league scoring title—Bobby Hull held the record in 1966 and Stan Mikita in the other four years.

PEGGY FLEMING 1968 OLYMPICS

At fifteen years old, Peggy Fleming won her first U.S. Senior Ladies' figure-skating championship. She went on to win the next four titles in a row. In the North American championships, Fleming finished second in 1965 and then first in 1967. She struggled to win the world championships in 1965—but came in third. After training hard, she won the championships for the next three years. People around the world cheered for America's figure-skating sweetheart.

In 1968, Fleming represented the U.S. at the Winter Olympics in Grenoble, France. She skated the performance of her life and was rewarded with the gold medal. She was an instant hero. After the Olympics, Fleming turned professional. She skated with such groups as the Ice Capades, Holiday on Ice, and Ice Follies.

Celtic Pride

The Boston Celtics dominated professional basketball in the 1960s. Led by stars such as Bill Russell, Tom Heinsohn, Frank Ramsey, and Bill Sharman, the team entered the sixties with a National Basketball Association championship and added another two in a row to their record.

In 1962, the Celtics seemed unbeatable. The team finished the regular season with a record sixty wins. No other professional team had finished the season so well. Russell was made the league MVP for the second time, becoming the first repeat award winner. In playoff competition, the Celtics met Wilt Chamberlain and the Philadelphia Warriors. In a close semifinal match-up, the Celtics managed to squeak by the Warriors and claimed another NBA championship. Every year, the Celtics fought their way to the top and won championship after championship. In 1966, they won their eighth straight NBA championship, something no other team had ever done. The following year, the streak ended. Wilt Chamberlain and the Los Angeles Lakers stole the crown from the Celtics after a two-point win.

Boston Celtics player Bill Russell handles the ball as Cincinnati Royals player Oscar Robertson attempts to guard him.

Iron Mike

At 122 pounds, Mike Ditka barely made his high school football team. By his senior year, he had gained 100 pounds and was a force to be feared on the field. He established himself as a linebacker, tight end, and one of the best punters in the country. Ditka also had a reputation for being intense and determined. This unstoppable quality earned him the nickname "Iron Mike."

In 1961, Ditka was a first-round draft choice of the Chicago Bears. His first season was one of the best ever by a National Football League tight end—he scored twelve touchdowns on fifty-six catches, gaining 1,076 yards. His incredible showing earned him the rookie of the year award. The years did not slow Ditka, either. In 1964, he tallied seventy-five catches, which was a record for tight ends at that time. In his six seasons with the Bears, Ditka made the All-Pro team four times.

A few trades in the late sixties left Ditka playing for the Dallas Cowboys. He helped the team win the Super Bowl in 1971. He retired the following year with a league-record of 427 career catches.

Muhammad Ali fought his way into history with a record of 56 wins—37 by way of knockout.

Surprise Champion

Cassius Clay was definitely the underdog in the 1964 heavyweight championship fight. Clay had won a gold medal at the Olympics, but boxing fans thought that the bigger and meaner Sonny Liston would easily defeat him. What people did not consider was that Clay was faster. The 22-year-old fighter knocked Liston out on February 25 with a punch that was so fast that many people missed it. American boxing fans went crazy for the new champion.

In 1964, Clay became a Muslim and changed his name to Muhammad Ali. When the Vietnam War draft board came calling, Ali refused to join the army because of his religious beliefs. He was stripped of his championship title as a result. In 1970, the fighter won a court appeal that reversed the decision. Four years later, Ali defeated George Foreman to reclaim his title as "the greatest." His dancing in the ring and his arrogance out of it excited the public, especially young African Americans. He became a role model for many young men.

Golfers Up to Par

Jack Nicklaus and Arnold Palmer were two of the best golfers ever. Palmer became the first golfer to win the Masters championship four times. He won in 1958, 1960, 1962, and 1964. He also dominated at the Open tournaments, winning the 1960 U.S. Open and the British Open in 1961 and 1962. By 1968, Palmer had become the first golfer to claim more than $1 million in prize money. Before this, golf had been a sport for the upper classes, but Palmer's personality and skill helped many "everyday" Americans enjoy the game. Palmer had a huge fan following, and "Arnie's Army" cheered him on. As the years passed, Palmer competed and won several Senior tournaments. He is one of the most successful and popular golfers in history.

Another talented golfer, Jack Nicklaus, won his first professional tournament at the U.S. Open in 1962, beating Arnold Palmer. "The Golden Bear" won six Masters tournaments, including ones in 1963, 1965, and 1966. He was the first golfer to ever win back-to-back Masters titles. Nicklaus also walked away with five Professional Golfers' Association championships starting in 1963, as well as three more U.S. Open titles in 1967, 1972, and 1980, and three British Open titles in 1966, 1970, and 1978. He went on to win numerous Senior tournaments and made a name for himself as a golf-course architect. *Golf Digest* voted ten of his designs to be in the top 100 golf courses in the U.S.

Jack Nicklaus holds up his winning trophy with the help of an old friend.

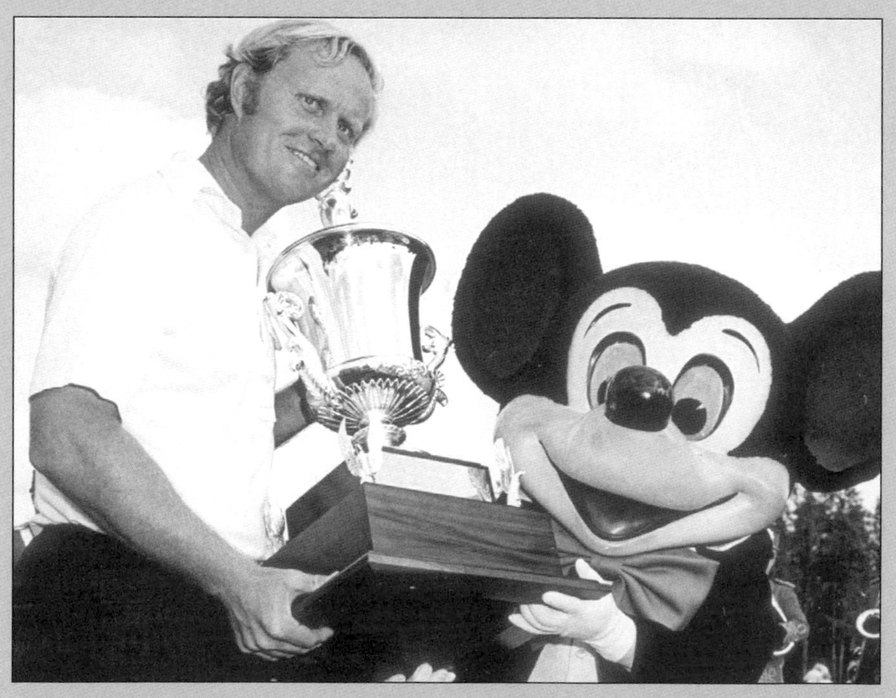

Bomb Shelters

American families watched in fear as the Cold War became worse in the 1960s. The possibility of a nuclear war was real, and people began preparing for it. In 1961, President Kennedy announced to Americans that if there was a Soviet nuclear attack, those families not directly hit by the blast and fires could survive in bomb shelters. Some people doubted that anyone would be able to survive a nuclear attack. Others decided that it was better to try to protect themselves. Across the country, people began to build **fallout** shelters. These shelters were often holes in the ground lined with concrete or steel. They were stocked with enough canned food and water for a two-week stay, as well as with games to pass the time. By the end of the year, tensions between the U.S. and the Soviet Union began to relax. Americans' nightmares about nuclear war and the need for bomb shelters lessened.

"There is no guarantee that any of your defenses—or even the nation's defenses—will be adequate if the enemy attacks all-out with complete surprise. But they will increase your odds."

Life magazine, September 15, 1961

Citizens take to the streets to protest racial inequality in the U.S.

Race Riots

Racial tensions sparked riots across the country. After an off-duty police officer killed a 15-year-old African-American boy in New York in July 1964, the African-American community exploded. Rioting began, as people hurled firebombs at police and white-owned businesses. The violence lasted for days and spread to Brooklyn. African Americans there continued to protest unfair treatment by police and authority figures. When the situation was brought under control, about a thousand people had been arrested, six lay dead, and hundreds had been wounded. On the other side of the country, the Los Angeles neighborhood of Watts also erupted with riots. It took 20,000 National Guardsmen five days to settle the community. Thirty-four people were killed, hundreds were injured, and damage totaled $40 million.

In 1967, the worst race riot in U.S. history broke out in Detroit. City police had raided a club where Black Power activists were known to meet. Seventy-five people were arrested. The African-American community viewed this as an attempt to undermine their fight for equality. For four days, fighting swept the city while the National Guard tried to ease the tension. In the end, thirty-eight people died and the city was left in ruins. Fires and looting totaled about $500 million in damages.

These riots prompted **militant** groups, including the Black Panthers, to take to the streets. The Black Panthers dressed in military clothing and carried rifles, creating fear both in the white community and with the authorities. Some such groups began pushing more for independence than for equality. It took a long time to reestablish trust between communities after the race wars of the sixties.

Watching Weight

In the sixties, miniskirts and other fashion crazes were designed for smaller-framed women. As a result, many people tried to thin down. In 1963, one woman's struggle with her weight resulted in a multimillion-dollar business. Thirty-nine-year-old Jean Nidetch found weight clinic plans difficult to stick to, so she decided to invite six friends to join her in trying to lose weight. They supported each other throughout the struggle. Nidetch was successful. Weighing in at 214 pounds, she lost 70 pounds in the first year. She then began using the group's techniques to help others. Nidetch and two friends created Weight Watchers Incorporated, which combined a diet of low fat and lots of fruit and vegetables with the morale-boosting weekly meetings. Within five years, Weight Watchers had spread to eighty-seven locations across the U.S. Since selling the company to food giant Heinz in the late 1970s, Weight Watchers franchises have popped up in twenty-four countries around the world.

Weight Watchers creator Jean Nidetch helped countless Americans win the battle of the bulge.

Society

I Have a Dream

In the late 1950s, Martin Luther King, Jr. launched a nonviolent campaign for equality. In April 1963, King organized desegregation marches in Birmingham, Alabama. He brought teenagers and young children into the peaceful demonstrations. The police commissioner ordered officers with attack dogs and firefighters with high-pressure water hoses to stop the marchers. Pictures of young protesters being attacked by dogs and knocked down by blasts of water were splashed on front pages and on newscasts around the world. King was arrested and briefly imprisoned for ignoring a court order against demonstrating.

Then, on August 28, about 300,000 people gathered outside the Lincoln Memorial to join King in the March on Washington. Here, he delivered his famous "I have a dream" speech. The peaceful crowd was marching for the right to an education, for employment, and for the right to eat and learn alongside white Americans. King's passion and skills as a speaker made many Americans rethink the issues. King was voted *Time* magazine's "Man of the Year" in 1963 and was awarded the Nobel Peace Prize in 1964.

Some groups did not like King's message, and he and his family were continually threatened and even attacked. On April 4, 1968, a drifter named James Earl Ray shot King at a Memphis hotel. His death devastated many Americans and resulted in a wave of violence across the country. The civil rights movement suffered further blows with the 1963 murder of activist Medgar Evers and the 1965 killing of Malcolm X, a leader who spoke for angry, urban African Americans.

FREEDOM RIDERS

A 1960 Supreme Court ruling stated that **segregation** was illegal in bus stations. People of all races were free to travel from state to state aboard the same buses. In 1961, the Congress of Racial Equality set out to test this ruling. In May, Freedom Riders boarded two buses in Washington and left for a tour of the South. One bus made it to Anniston, Alabama, before being stoned and firebombed. Some riders were beaten. The other bus was attacked in Montgomery, Alabama. The state government did not try to stop the attacks. President Kennedy stepped in to ensure the safety of the passengers. The riders continued to Jackson, Mississippi, where they were arrested and jailed. By the end of the summer, over 300 Freedom Riders had risked their safety in an effort to achieve racial equality and desegregation.

Economy

Steel Trouble

In his first year as president, John F. Kennedy took part in negotiations between major steel companies and their workers. Kennedy wanted to keep labor costs down so that the companies could keep their prices at a steady level. By the end of 1962, the parties decided that workers' wages would remain the same but that their benefits would be increased. With this deal, Kennedy assumed that steel companies would not raise their prices. He was wrong. Two weeks later, the president of U.S. Steel announced a price increase of $6 per ton. Kennedy viewed this as a betrayal. He attacked the action and launched a grand jury investigation on price fixing in the steel business. Three days later, several steel companies reduced their prices. By April 14, U.S. Steel had reduced their prices, too.

The production of steel is a major U.S. industry.

While Kennedy came out on top, the situation hurt relationships between the government and businesses. Kennedy's battle against the steel companies confirmed American businesspeople's view that Kennedy and the Democrats were not friendly toward big business. Kennedy's hard work during the previous year to convince people otherwise was wasted.

THE NEW FRONTIER

President Kennedy spoke about the New Frontier. His plan was to create a steady and high rate of economic growth in the U.S. He asked for medical coverage for senior citizens, more money set aside for education, the responsible use of natural resources, and housing and community development. While some of his economic efforts failed, he fought for others and won. He raised the national minimum wage from $1.00 to $1.25 over four years. He also increased the number of workers affected by the legislation by 3.5 million. President Kennedy promised to cut **tariffs** by 50 percent over a 5-year period and to get rid of the tax altogether on some items. This policy was prompted by the quickly developing European Union. The U.S. had to remain competitive in trade, and the lifted taxes allowed the U.S. to trade freely with countries in Europe.

Boosting the Economy

President Kennedy tried to jump-start the economy in the early 1960s. In 1962, prices on the New York Stock Exchange dropped dramatically. It was the sharpest decline since the 1929 market crash that had started the Great Depression. Kennedy began taking measures to help businesses prosper. By 1963, he had proposed an enormous tax cut. He wanted to slash taxes by more than $10 billion, which also included lowering business taxes. He wanted people to feel confident in the economy and keep spending money. If they were taxed less, citizens would have more to spend. An increased minimum wage was geared at giving Americans a bit more cash in their pockets. The extra spending would then encourage new businesses, and the taxes brought in from the expanded economy would make up for the loss from the initial cut. Many Americans supported these efforts, but some still insisted that the government was anti-business, especially after Kennedy's hard line with the steel industry.

War on Poverty

In 1964, President Johnson declared war on poverty in the U.S. His economic program called for a system to help people in areas of extreme poverty. This system included such safety nets as greater access to food stamps and unemployment payments. Johnson called for a youth program that would help get young Americans into the workforce—part of the "job corps." There needed to be special assistance to schools, libraries, hospitals, and nursing homes so that all Americans would be part of the solution. Johnson asked Congress for $962 million to put his plan to fight poverty into action. At the same time, he began cutting in other areas, including the Defense Department and Atomic Energy Commission projects. He managed to trim about $2 billion, which enabled him to add small amounts to his poverty program. This was one war the U.S. public could get behind.

"Unfortunately, many Americans live on the outskirts of hope—some because of their poverty, some because of their color, and all too many because of both."

President Lyndon Johnson

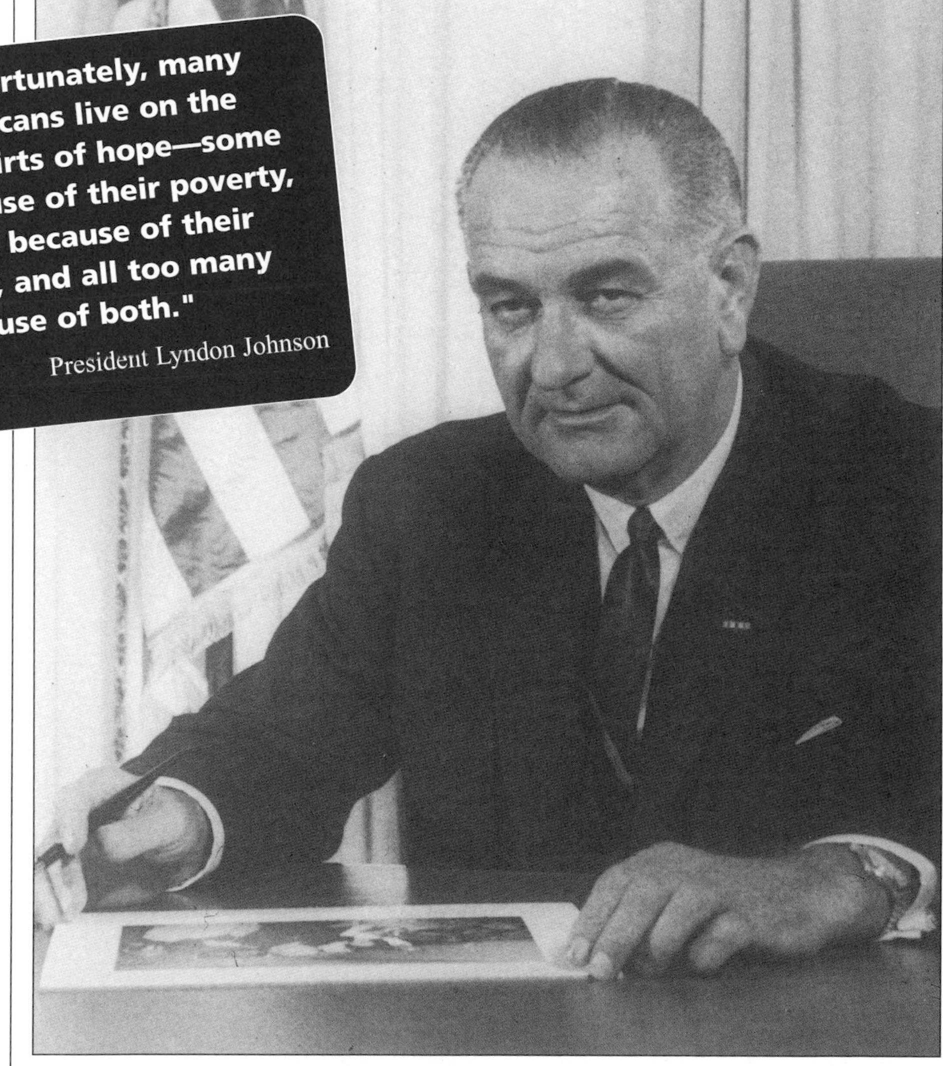

President Johnson's war on poverty was a strong statement to the American people. Throughout his time in office, he stood up for the workers by creating new jobs and expanding social programs.

Flower Power

In the mid-sixties, the hippie look took hold of the U.S. Beehive hairdos were out and bone-straight hairstyles became the rage. Women even ironed their hair to achieve the straightest style possible. Men and women favored long hair that draped around their faces and down their backs.

The "flower power" of the sixties was everywhere. People wore flowers in their hair and painted or embroidered flowers on their shirts and faded bell-bottomed jeans. Skirts that flowed to their feet were an essential part of a female hippie's wardrobe. Shoes were optional, as many hippies preferred to be "at one with nature" and walk around barefoot. Also, these people were the first to wear T-shirts as outerwear, but they went further than that. They tie-dyed the shirts with spirals and splashes of vibrant colors. This style would forever be associated with the peace-and-love generation of the sixties.

Peace signs and a belief in "flower power" were common throughout the sixties.

Twiggy Style

Leslie Hornby's classmates called her "Sticks" because of her small frame and boyish figure. Then, at 17 years of age, the British girl captured the attention of the fashion industry. Now called Twiggy, she became the world's first supermodel. She arrived in the U.S. in 1967, where she was met at the airport by flashing cameras and adoring fans. Americans had not seen such a reception since the Beatles invaded earlier in the decade. With her bobbed hair, false eyelashes, and bean-pole, **waifish** figure, Twiggy became a symbol of innocence and youth. Some were uncomfortable about the 5-foot, 6-inch, 91-pound star representing the ideal look. Still, that would not stop Americans from following her lead. Her trendsetting clothing line could not keep up with the demand for her short dresses, knit tops, and striped stockings. Dolls, lunchboxes, posters, trading cards, and other goods were quickly produced as the Twiggy look swept the country. She retired at the end of the sixties, but not before becoming a fashion **icon**.

Twiggy's international style set the stage for future supermodels.

SHORT SKIRTS

In 1965, less really was more. French designer André Courreges sent models onto the runway in high white boots and skirts that rested four inches above the knee. This scandalous design surprised the audience into silence. But not for long. Soon, women cheered for the miniskirt, though often they could not afford it. Then British designer Mary Quant brought runway styles to ordinary people. She not only made her styles more affordable, she also made them shorter. Her stores sold out of the radical new style every day. She sewed all night to keep up with the demand. Courrèges soon realized that there was a market for everyday fashion for women. He made his styles available to anyone daring enough to wear them. Millions of American women did so throughout the rest of the decade.

The Beatle Invasion

The Beatles were discovered in a Liverpool pub and became the most popular British musicians in history. In 1964, John Lennon, Paul McCartney, George Harrison, and Ringo Starr invaded North America with more than just their remarkable musical talents. They brought their style with them, too. During their U.S. tour, the Beatles, with their unbeatable harmonies and masterfully written songs, appeared on *The Ed Sullivan Show*. They also sported their signature bowl-cut hairstyles and matching suits. Everywhere they went they were greeted by screaming teenagers. The shaggy hairstyles that fell over their ears swept America as quickly as Beatlemania did. As the sixties rolled on and hippies became popular, the Beatles' image changed, and Americans were eager to keep up with their trendsetting styles. By the time the band broke up in 1970, they had established themselves as rock-and-roll legends.

The Beatles celebrate after receiving their Member of the British Empire medals in 1965.

Immigration

Revised Immigration Act

On October 13, 1965, President Johnson signed the Immigration Act in a ceremony on Ellis Island. The location was fitting because Ellis Island had once housed the headquarters of the Immigration and Naturalization Department. The Act was a collection of changes to the 1952 immigration law. It removed national origins as a determining factor in immigration. Each year, about 120,000 people were allowed to come into the U.S. from countries in the Western Hemisphere, and 170,000 people could come from the rest of the world. This was the first time that the number of immigrants from the West was capped. It was to regulate the number of people entering the U.S. from Latin America. Also, no more than 20,000 people from one country could seek citizenship in one year. The Act attempted to include refugees in the plan by setting aside about 17,400 openings per year for them. Immediately after the Act was passed, immigration to the U.S. increased.

"The bill will not flood our cities with immigrants. It will not upset the ethnic mix of our society."

Senator Edward Kennedy

Braceros Debate

Since the 1940s, temporary immigrants were allowed to come to the U.S. to work on the farms. What started as a wartime issue of employee shortages had carried on until the 1960s. Many organized labor unions and other groups wanted President Kennedy to put a stop to these workers, called braceros. Farmers defended the system, as did the Mexican government. They said that it was a beneficial and important policy. If it did not exist, they said, it would be difficult for them to do business. A representative of the National Cotton Council told a committee that Americans were unwilling to engage in the type of work needed to harvest many crops. They needed the Mexican braceros to staff their businesses. Mexico wanted the policy to continue because much of the money braceros earned was sent back to their families in Mexico. As the fifties ran into the sixties, support for the agreement decreased. Some government officials said that the practice would have stopped if it were not for diplomatic complications with Mexico. By 1964, the use of braceros was halted. This was partly due to concerns about American workers losing jobs because of braceros. It was also partly due to the mechanization of farm work through the 1950s and 1960s. From start to finish, immigration officials calculated that about 4 million temporary workers had been recruited into the braceros program.

Mexican braceros cross into Texas to work for U.S. farmers.

Act Opens Door to New Immigrants

The Immigration Act of 1965 allowed more categories of immigrants to gain entry into the U.S. New immigrants could bring their spouses and children with them. Family members claimed as much as 74 percent of the available places after the Act was underway. The revised Act also added parents of adult U.S. citizens to the list of people who could immigrate. Unmarried sons and daughters of U.S. citizens could now claim up to 20 percent of the total places available to immigrants.

As the family relationship became more distant, so did the level of **preference** given to the applicants. Brothers and sisters of citizens, for example, were given fifth preference. Skilled laborers had previously been given special preference and up to half of the available places. Now they were sixth preference, behind professionals, artists, and scientists, who were third preference. The relaxed immigration policy showed in the number of immigrants entering the U.S. From July 1, 1960, to June 30, 1968, about 259,000 immigrants entered the country each year. Once the Act was in full swing, from July 1968, to June 1976, the number jumped to 391,000 per year.

President Johnson signs the Immigration Act into law.

NEWCOMERS

Between 1961 and 1970, more than 3.1 million people legally immigrated to the U.S. They came from all over the world. Below is a breakdown of where some of these new Americans came from, along with their estimated numbers.

Caribbean	470,200
Mexico	453,900
Canada	413,300
South America	257,900
Italy	214,100
Great Britain	213,800

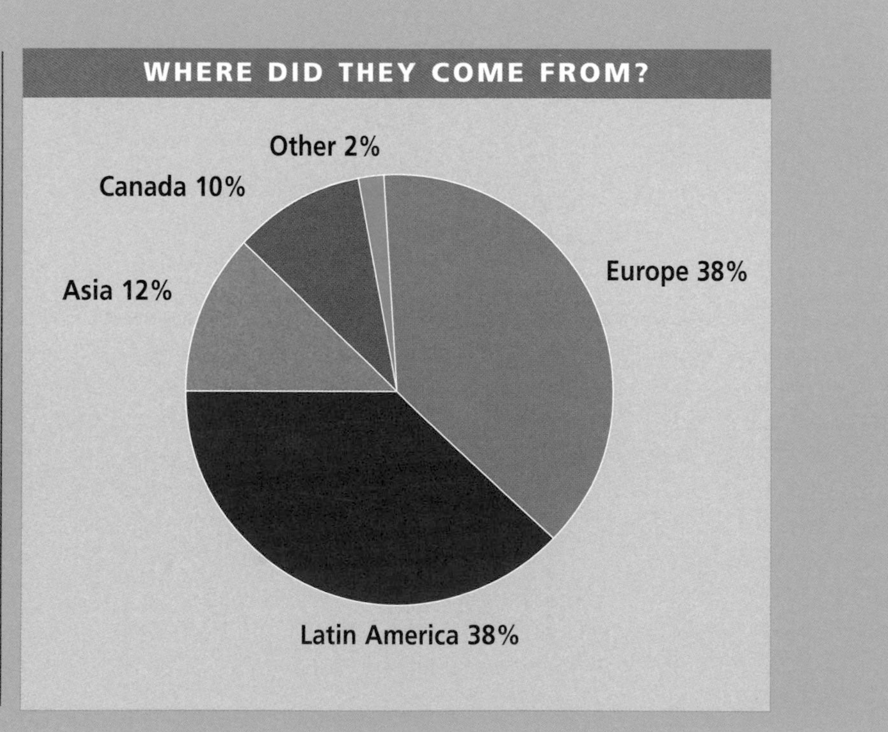

Florence Ballard, Mary Wilson, and Diana Ross made the Supremes a sensation.

Supremely Talented

Diana Ross, Mary Wilson, and Florence Ballard were teenagers from a Detroit housing project. With the help of Berry Gordy's Motown recording label, they became the Supremes in 1961. Gordy dressed the women exactly alike and made Diana Ross's vocals most prominent. Their first few songs were forgettable, but their 1964 song, "Where Did Our Love Go," hit number one. Twelve more number-one hits followed over the next six years, including "Stop! In the Name of Love" and "Baby Love." The Supremes appealed to a wide section of society. The Supremes blurred racial differences by topping all of *Billboard* magazine's charts. In 1967, Gordy renamed the group "Diana Ross and the Supremes," and he replaced Florence Ballard with Cindy Birdsong. The songwriting team chiefly responsible for the group's success left Motown and started their own record company. This left the Supremes struggling for quality songs. In January 1970, the hit group gave its last performance, and Diana Ross left to pursue a solo career.

Grateful Dead

The Grateful Dead created a new kind of performance when they formed their group in 1965. Their style of rock music became known as psychedelic rock. They played without a set list of songs. Instead, they did things on the spur of the moment, adapting to whatever the audience liked the best. The Dead quickly established an enormous following of fans, called Deadheads, who tailed the band from concert to concert. The leader of The Grateful Dead, Jerry Garcia, was a hero to many of the group's fans. Over the course of the next thirty years, The Grateful Dead released several hit albums, including *Anthem of the Sun* in 1968, their first live album called *Live Dead* in 1970, and *Workingman's Dead* in 1970. The Dead performed countless live shows and concerts and toured widely for decades. They have become the highest-grossing live band in rock history.

FOLK HEROES

The sweetheart of folk music was Joan Baez. Shortly after her appearance on the folk scene, Baez became a symbol of her generation. Her clear and simple songs attracted enormous crowds to the folk festivals and concerts at which she performed. She protested the Vietnam War not only through her songs but also through her actions. She refused to pay taxes that supported the military effort in Vietnam. She also founded international organizations to promote human rights and other causes. Baez and folk hero Bob Dylan often sang together at music festivals.

Bob Dylan's raspy voice became the voice of the sixties. He wrote songs that told what his generation was feeling and thinking. "Blowin' in the Wind" (1962) and "The Times They Are A-Changin'" (1964) made him the undisputed king of folk protest songs.

Woodstock Shock

Not even the organizers knew how many people would show up at the outdoor music festival in 1969. The "Three Days of Peace and Music" drew more than 400,000 people to a farm in Bethel, New York, between August 15 and 17. Most of the people joining the Woodstock party were young—hippies, students, and war protesters. The hottest musicians of the time, including Jimi Hendrix, Janis Joplin, Santana, and The Grateful Dead, performed in the searing heat and pouring rain.

The weather was just one of the problems. The unexpected turnout meant that there were not sufficient facilities for so many people. Traffic into the farm was backed up for miles, making it difficult to get supplies and musicians into the venue. Helicopters dropped the bands on stage and picked them up again. Food was also airlifted into the area. Some local residents helped out by setting up soup kitchens to feed the thousands of young people. Despite the rain and lack of food and washrooms, the spirit of Woodstock prevailed. People took the problems in stride, played in the mud, danced to the music, and became an important part of sixties history.

Beach Boys

The three Wilson brothers, their cousin Mike Love, and their friend Al Jardine became the Beach Boys in 1961. They did not intend to become superstars—they sang because they loved to. They sang about the beach, surfing, being young and in love, and the joys of experiencing it all. Brian, one of the brothers, was the main songwriter and producer, and his father, Murray, managed the band. Brian helped shape what would become known as surf music. The group's talent launched them into superstardom with a string of hit songs, including "Surfin' USA" (1963), "Help Me, Rhonda" (1965), and "California Girls" (1965). The Beach Boys moved into the international spotlight, but the band's music lasted longer than the band. In 1964, Brian Wilson suffered a nervous breakdown and quit performing in public. The band released *Pet Sounds* in 1966, which the critics praised but the public did not buy. Still, this album has had a major influence on other performers. Paul McCartney credits it with inspiring one of the Beatles' hit albums, *Sgt. Pepper's Lonely Heart Club Band.*

The Beach Boys were inducted into the Rock and Roll Hall of Fame in 1998 and the Vocal Group Hall of Fame in 1998. They continued to tour and perform into the 21st century.

Dennis Wilson, Al Jardine, Mike Love, Brian Wilson, and Carl Wilson made up the superstar singing group the Beach Boys.

Spy Disaster

The relationship between the Soviet Union and the U.S. was at an all-time low in the sixties. Throughout the fifties, U.S. spy planes had flown over the Soviet Union, but the USSR could not do anything about it. Their early missiles did not have the power to reach the planes. By the sixties, technology had advanced, and the Soviets had caught up to the U-2 planes. On May 1, 1960, Central Intelligence Agency pilot Gary Powers was shot down while flying over the Soviet Union in a spy plane. President Eisenhower and his government tried to explain away the incident, which came at a terrible time. It was a few weeks before a Four Powers summit meeting was to take place in Paris. The Cold War became a few degrees colder.

Premier Khrushchev made an announcement on May 5, but he did not say that the pilot had been taken from the wreckage alive. U.S. officials tried to claim that the aircraft was a civilian one that had accidentally entered Soviet airspace. Then the premier played his ace-in-the-hole. Powers had confessed to spying. Eisenhower tried to patch things up enough to move ahead with the Paris summit, but not even the promise of no more U-2 spy planes could appease Khrushchev. He suggested that Eisenhower be **impeached**. The summit was called off. Powers was tried for spying and sentenced to ten years in a Soviet prison. Many Americans did not feel sorry for him—they did not respect that he had confessed and pleaded guilty to the charges. Regardless, in 1962, the U.S. government traded Powers for the Soviet spy Rudolph Abel, who had been arrested in the U.S.

Gary Powers attends a senate hearing holding a model of his spy plane.

No Nukes

Relations between the Soviet Union and Communist China had begun to sour, and the U.S. took advantage of the situation and reopened communications with the USSR. The Soviets decided to help ease international tensions about nuclear war, especially after the Cuban Missile Crisis. On August 5, 1963, the U.S., Britain, and the Soviet Union agreed on a treaty that would ban atomic weapons testing in the atmosphere, in space, and underwater. Testing underground, however, was not banned. President Kennedy and Premier Khrushchev installed a "hot line" for easy communication between the two countries. In case of an emergency, the two heads of state could contact each other directly. This agreement helped calm fears of nuclear disaster in the U.S. and around the world. It also brought the feuding countries a step closer together.

"We all inhabit this small planet. We all breathe the same air. We all cherish our children's future, and we are all mortal."

John F. Kennedy, on the coming together of the U.S. and the Soviet Union

U.S.–JAPAN TREATY

The close relationship between Japan and the U.S. after World War II caused tension between Japan and communist countries. In 1960, the U.S. and Japan met to renegotiate the 1952 mutual-security treaty. This had been signed after Japan had reclaimed its sovereignty. The revised agreement stated that the U.S. could keep its military bases in Japan and could become involved against foreign or communist aggression in the area. Many Japanese people were against the treaty because it made a trade relationship with Japan's communist neighbors nearly impossible. Demonstrations flared as students protested Japanese support of U.S. foreign policy.

Dominican Republic

On April 24, 1965, an army group rebelled against the government of the Dominican Republic. Four days later, U.S. marines landed in the area. Many American citizens lived there, so President Johnson sent 22,000 U.S. troops to the country to protect them. The troops were also there to prevent a Communist government from taking control of the country. U.S. forces stationed themselves between the rebel-occupied parts of Santo Domingo and the areas run by government loyalists. In May, a cease-fire was established, and U.S. troops took on peacekeeping duties. The following month, the marines left the Dominican Republic, but 12,500 other soldiers stayed. The U.S. presence in the Dominican Republic caused anti-American feelings in many parts of the world, and many people within the U.S. criticized the decision to enter the country as well.

U.S. Army forces patrol the streets of Santa Domingo, Dominican Republic, to guard against rebel arms shipments.

Failed Peace in Vietnam

President Johnson tried to move ahead with peace negotiations to end the Vietnam War in 1968. He had little success. The peace talks in Paris broke down in May after disagreements about the status of the National Liberation Front (NLF), a communist group in South Vietnam. The South Vietnamese government in Saigon refused to recognize the NLF.

In October, just before the U.S. presidential election, candidate Hubert Humphrey pushed for a peace settlement. Richard Nixon secretly convinced South Vietnamese President Nguyen Van Thieu to wait for better terms that would materialize once Nixon was elected. Thieu announced that he would not negotiate with communists, bringing the peace talks to a screeching halt. Nixon did not have any more luck when he took over the peace talks. Neither side would alter its position. The communists insisted that all U.S. troops leave Vietnam. They also demanded that the Saigon government be removed and replaced via an election that included the NLF government party. Peace talks fell apart and both sides continued fighting the war.

VIETNAM
LAOS
Haiphong
South China Sea
Da Nang
THAILAND
N
CAMBODIA
Saigon
South China Sea
N
0 200 miles

The U.S spent more than $150 billion fighting the war in Vietnam.

Scrambled Names

Unscramble the following sixties celebrities:

1. RELTAW TECKIRON
2. LASRECH LEDGLEAU
3. DORNAL MALPRE
4. ELLSIE RHYNOB
5. RABIN LINSOW

Answers:
1. Walter Cronkite
2. Charles De Gaulle
3. Arnold Palmer
4. Leslie Hornby
5. Brian Wilson

Multiple Choice

1 The *Eagle* was:
- a) a sixties dance craze.
- b) the craft that landed Neil Armstrong on the moon.
- c) Captain Kirk's nickname.

2 Algeria's fight for independence was:
- a) defeated quickly.
- b) granted immediately by France.
- c) one of the longest independence struggles ever fought by a European power.

3 The Gulf of Tonkin was:
- a) the location of alleged attacks by Vietnam on U.S. ships.
- b) a resort in Persia.
- c) a peace negotiation.

4 Audrey Hepburn:
- a) made hundreds of movies until she was in her eighties.
- b) won an Academy Award for *Breakfast at Tiffany's*.
- c) retired at the end of the decade when she was on top.

5 The Peace Corps:
- a) was a peacekeeping unit used to end wars.
- b) sent volunteers overseas to help Third World and developing countries.
- c) was dismantled in 1966.

Answers: 1. b); 2. c); 3. a); 4. c); 5. b).

True or False

1. Americans were the first astronauts in space.
2. Most young people in the 1960s were hippies.
3. John F. Kennedy and Richard Nixon were the first candidates to argue their platforms in front of television cameras.
4. The 1964 Civil Rights Act eased racial tensions in the U.S.
5. Many U.S. families were scared of nuclear war and built shelters to protect themselves.

Answers:
1. False. The Soviet Union sent the first person into space in 1961. Americans did not travel in space until the following year;
2. False. Most young people were not hippies, but the hippie style and attitudes had a huge impact on society and fashion;
3. True;
4. False. Race riots and demonstrations continued throughout the decade;
5. True.

Newsmakers

Match the person or people in the news with their story!

1. Jean Nidetch
2. Andy Warhol
3. Ronald Ridenhour
4. Sidney Poitier
5. Adolf Eichmann
6. Harper Lee
7. Tommy Smith
8. Alexander Dubcek
9. Gary Powers
10. Jerry Garcia

a) led Prague Spring
b) wrote *To Kill a Mockingbird*
c) African-American Olympian
d) leader of the Grateful Dead
e) pop artist
f) spy pilot caught in the Soviet Union
g) started Weight Watchers
h) first African American to win a best actor Oscar
i) convicted for murder in My Lai tragedy
j) Holocaust war criminal

Answers: 1. g); 2. e); 3. i); 4. h); 5. j); 6. b); 7. c); 8. a); 9. f); 10. d).

USA 1960s Glossary

allegedly: according to a statement or accusation often made without proof

appealed: took the case to a higher court for review

capitalism: an economic system in which private owners control trade and industry for profit

Cold War: a long competition between the U.S. and the Soviet Union

communist: someone who follows the economic system whereby property is owned by the community and each member works for the common good

cosmonaut: a Soviet astronaut

coup: an action to overthrow the government

desegregating: removing laws that keep people of different races apart

exiles: people who had been sent away from their home country

fallout: lasting debris from a nuclear explosion

Gestapo: Nazi Germany's secret police

Holocaust: the systematic killing of millions of Jews by Nazi forces in World War II

icon: a symbol or representative

impeached: charged with misconduct as a public official

incriminating: evidence of being criminally involved.

inflammation: redness, heat, and pain caused by the body

militant: prepared to take aggressive action for a cause

mutinied: rebelled against authority, especially by members of the armed forces against their officers

preference: favoring one over another

rapport: a positive relationship between people

reconnaissance: an examination of an area to gather information about it

sadistic: the enjoyment of watching or inflicting pain or cruelty

segregation: separation of racial groups

socialist: a person who supports the economic system whereby society as a whole controls the means of production

sovereignty: independence

tariffs: fixed taxes on imports and exports

urban renewal: giving cities new opportunities to grow

Vietcong: a member of the communist guerrilla forces in Vietnam

waifish: like a helpless person or abandoned child

USA 1960s

Learning More

Here are some book resources and Internet links if you want to learn more about the people, places, and events that made headlines during the 1960s.

Books

Anderson, Christopher. *The Book of People*. New York: G.P. Putnam's Sons, 1981.

Brewster, Todd and Peter Jennings. *The Century for Young People*. New York: Random House Inc., 1999.

Sendak, Maurice. *Where the Wild Things Are.* New York: HarperCollins, 1963.

Internet Links

www.historyplace.com/kennedy/gallery.htm

www.bbhq.com/sixties2.htm

www.sixtiespop.freeserve.co.uk

For information about other U.S. subjects, type your key words into a search engine such as Alta Vista or Yahoo!

USA 1960s

Index